THE GOLDEN AGE
OF STYLE

THE GOLDEN AGE OF STYLE

Julian Robinson

Orbis Publishing

LONDON

Orbis   Golden Age   disk 16   4831

Title page: A drawing by George Barbier
from a design by Worth. It was entitled
'*Des Roses Dans La Nuit*' and appeared
in the August 1921 edition of the
Gazette du Bon Ton
This page: One of Paul Allier's
illustrations for *Les Fleurs*

The illustrations in this book come from
Julian Robinson's collection of fashion
plates and magazines except for the
following: 10 (bottom) Mary Evans Picture
Library; 10 (top) Royal Museum of Fine
Arts, Copenhagen; 11 (left) IGDA/photo
Buscaglia; 11 (right) photo John Webb;
12 (bottom) British Film Institute

ⓒ 1976 by Orbis Publishing Limited
First published in Great Britain by
Orbis Publishing Limited, London 1976

Reprinted 1983, 1985
Printed in Italy
ISBN 0-85613-548-8

Contents

Preface

9 Introduction
The Artists and the Illustrations   by Barbara Baines

30 The Age of Opulence 1901-1911

40 Art Déco Revolution 1911-1919

68 The Golden Age of Style 1919-1925

92 A New Fashion Image 1925-1932

114 The End of an Epoch 1932-1939

Collections

Bibliography

Index

Preface

Earlier this century a completely new style of design was created in fashion and the decorative arts in western Europe, reaching its peak just over fifty years ago with the Paris Exhibition of Decorative Arts in 1925. This important exhibition aimed to promote the new style, which combined the luxury of beautiful materials with artistic excellence. Later it became known as *Art Déco*, a term which has been used very loosely in recent years, often in relation to cheap manufactured goods which in no way live up to the original ideals of the movement.

The development of *Art Déco* was promoted throughout the world during its 'golden years' by a number of high-quality hand-printed books, magazines, albums and periodicals which were published in the twenty-five years between 1908–1932. These publications, with their insight, wit, accuracy, artistry and ingenuity, captured the true spirit of this 'golden age of style', recording it and preserving it in all its glory for future generations to enjoy.

This book recaptures that 'golden age', as seen through the eyes of the artists, designers and reporters who worked on the outstanding publications of the period. In order to illustrate the differing aesthetic ideals of the refined luxury of *Art Déco*, the visual opulence of the *Belle Époque* and the plain functional styles of 'New Modernism', I have also referred to examples from the popular press of England, France and the United States from the turn of the century to the outbreak of the Second World War. The excitement of the finest publications is evoked by a hundred of the most colourful illustrations, chosen from my extensive collection. These illustrations have been selected from the most fruitful period of this 'golden age of style', when the very best pictorial artists worked in close co-operation with the leading dressmakers, jewellers, furriers, furniture-makers, fabric printers and milliners. The pictures they produced were designed as a true mirror of the age, giving a complete picture of contemporary life.

After working on the text and selecting the illustrations, I was more impressed than ever at the extraordinary inventiveness, elegance and quality of the illustrations, together with the unique designs they depicted. As a tribute to this achievement I have decided to dedicate this book to all the talented individuals who worked on those numerous publications, together with the artists, designers and craftsmen who created the fashions illustrated, the aesthetic quality of which may unfortunately never be seen again. I hope therefore that this book will stand as a fitting epitaph to this 'golden age of style'.

JULIAN ROBINSON

Left: An illustration by George Barbier of a design by Beer. It appeared in the October 1922 edition of the *Gazette du Bon Ton*

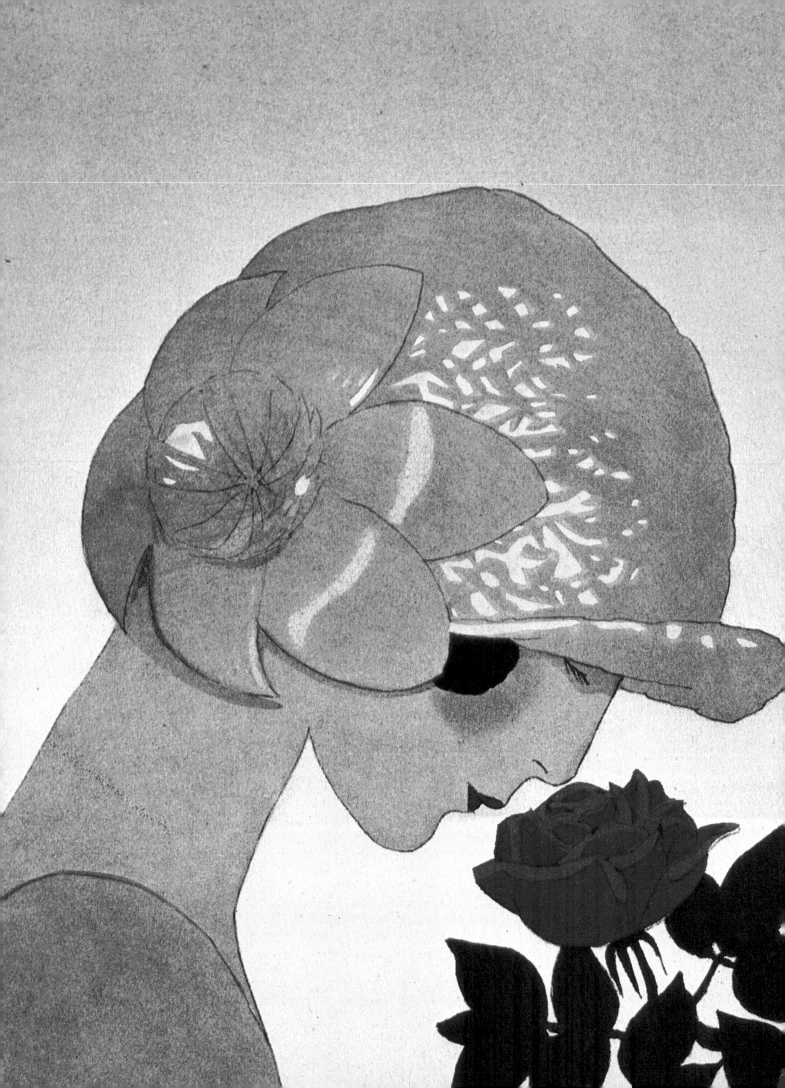

Introduction

The Artists and the Illustrations
by Barbara Baines

The art of fashion illustration had developed fitfully through the nineteenth century. Many illustrations reached high standards using engraving methods of reproduction. Others were technically poor or visually dull and clichéd. Nearly all were compromised by the need to convey with great clarity details of garment construction, the number of buttons and the texture of the fabrics and the appropriate accessories, at the expense of the atmosphere and vivacity of the figures they depicted. But, as the purpose of these illustrations was to inform the public of fashions and how to wear them, nothing more was expected of them.

Occasionally an artist of the calibre of Charles Dana Gibson, for example, would refresh the art with his particularly fine, lively hand and observant eye, but generally fashion illustration concentrated on detail, on information rather than expression; it developed its own linear language to cope with its particular job and remained isolated from any replenishment or influence from the mainstream

Left: Hat by Marthe Collot; painting by André Marty. *Gazette du Bon Ton*, June 1924. Some of the features which first appeared in fashion illustration before the First World War continued to be used for their evocative quality, such as the entirely empty background and the cut-out appearance of the silhouette

9

of the visual arts. Indeed, there was little chance for fashion illustrators to experiment when the problem of their obviously limited function was compounded by the frequent use of several artists to produce one drawing.

Team illustration was common practice, and survived alongside the high quality illustrations of the new school, which are shown in this book, just as dull photographic images in modern mail order catalogues survive alongside the more attractive pictures in prestigious fashion magazines. In 1918, a full decade after the first revolutionary album of fashion illustration *Les Robes de Paul Poiret* by Paul Iribe, this description of more traditional methods was written by Ethel Traphagen in her book *Costume Design and Illustration.* 'There is often a special artist who does nothing but layouts, grouping the figures and planning the page; another who makes sketches of the garments; another who draws them on the laidout figures; another who puts on the large washes; another who does details such as lace and embroidery; another who finishes the heads and still another who finishes the hands and feet.'

Small wonder, then, that in 1908 the *haute couturier* Paul Poiret saw the need for more expressive and interesting illustration, and that Paul Iribe seized the chance he offered. One artist, one album; the result was a cohesive and original style of illustration, which charmed the clients and greatly influenced his fellow illustrators.

Above left: *Madame Matisse*, painted in 1905 by Matisse, was one of the paintings exhibited in Paris which that year earned for him and his friends the name of *Fauves* or 'Wild Beasts'. Broad brush strokes of bright colour and the new treatment of the picture surface and of the human figure in pictures such as this shocked the public but refreshed and influenced the outlook of other artists, including fashion illustrators

Left: This page from a late nineteenth century issue of *Ladies Magazine* typifies problems in the style of illustration at that time. Although the elaborate ornament of the dresses is clearly shown, the characterization of the figures is weak, the background is ill-defined and the picture conveys very little atmosphere of its own. By contrast the illustrators of the early twentieth century brought life to their designs by looking outwards to the other arts for inspiration

Despite the fact that the drawings did not indicate the whereabouts of every seam or button, or perhaps because of this omission, they were minor works of art in their own right. Poiret followed this innovation by commissioning Georges Lepape to do another album in 1911. When that was completed fashion illustration was well on the way to entirely new pastures.

That this renaissance in fashion illustration should happen when and where it did is not, with hindsight, really surprising. It was almost inevitable. Fashion design, illustration and fashion journalism were, and still are, taken far more seriously in France than elsewhere. Poiret himself must take a major share of the credit, for he commissioned young and hitherto unknown illustrators, and

Below: Costume design by Léon Bakst for Diaghilev's Ballet Russe, to be worn by Vaslav Nijinsky in the Paris performance of *Le Dieu Bleu* in 1912. Bakst's exotic and richly-coloured set and costume designs caused great excitement when they were first seen in Paris in 1909. The *couturier* Poiret firmly denied he was influenced in any way by Bakst, but there are nevertheless many obvious parallels in their designs

Right: A late eighteenth century print by the Japanese artist Eishi, depicting two courtesans. Many features of Japanese art were used by fashion illustrators in the early 1920s, including a background left entirely plain or filled with grid-like screens and walls, figures grouped into fluid, curving shapes, overhanging foliage delicately painted, subtle colour combinations, and a general airiness associated with the Japanese 'floating world'

Left: From *Les Robes de Paul Poiret* by Iribe, published in 1908 to promote Poiret's *couture* collection of that year. Iribe's new approach included the use of empty backgrounds, of unshaded blocks of colour and a more interesting grouping of the figures

Right: One of Paul Poiret's turban designs, in *Les Choses de Paul Poiret* illustrated by Georges Lepape in 1911. This bold composition includes new and more subtle colour contrasts, and represents a fusion of many different style sources, ranging from oriental art to the pale petulant faces flickering on the cinema screens of the day

Below: A photograph of Norma Talmadge, taken on the set of one of the pre-1914 *Vitagraph* 'Belinda' films. Her soulful, pale face, emphasized by very heavy eye make-up and darkened lips, is very similar to those which began to appear in the pre-1914 fashion illustrations, such as the one by Georges Lepape shown on the right

gingered up the Paris *couture* world with great panache. He wrote later in his autobiography: '. . . when I began to do what I wanted to do in dress designing, there were absolutely no tints left on the palette of the colourists. . . . I threw into this sheep-cote a few rough wolves; reds, green, violets, royal blues, that made all the rest sing aloud.'

The first twenty-five years of the century was a period of rapid expansion and change in fashion and the world of *haute couture* which provided a sympathetic and stimulating environment for the innovations in fashion illustration. Between 1900 and 1925, for example, at least twenty new *haute couture* houses started up business in Paris, while the export of *haute couture* items, particularly *lingerie*, was a major and officially recognized and organized part of the French war effort between 1914 and 1918. The Great War accelerated the acquisition of managerial and technical skills in the manufacture of ready-to-wear clothes, because of the pressure to produce vast numbers of military uniforms quickly. Consequently the ready-to-wear industry had a boost to its development in the post-war years, which in turn gave even more *kudos* to *haute couture* clothes. And by an odd twist, the early loss

Right: A painting by Drian in *Gazette du Bon Ton*, June 1915, which neatly summed up the contrast between the luxurious, meticulous products of the *haute couture* workshops and the grim realities of the war shown by the map of military operations. Such flower-like fragility in a dress was never seen in the more bulbous fashions of the *Belle Époque*

Far right: The tubular, high-waisted evening dress which was worn by fashionable women was shown at its most provocative in this page by Georges Lepape, in the 1912 *Modes et Manières d'Aujourd'hui*. Not only did he reveal the shoulder and bust of the model, but he painted them in pale grey, a sharp contrast with the bright dress and the orange lighted-window, coloured as gaily as a Fauvist canvas. Lepape played on other contrasts too, with all the cool sensuality of a Japanese print: bare skin next to fur, curves set against straight lines, and a woman caught in reflective pose just before she plunges, alone, into the party

in the war of the northern cloth manufacturing areas to the enemy, and the need to conserve all heavy duty fabrics for the troops, hastened the fashionable woman's acceptance of a softer, slimmer silhouette which had been promoted by Paul Poiret and the fashion illustrators before the War.

Sensitive observers had noted a need for change and novelty and a certain restlessness beginning before the War, when fashion illustration was first launched on its new career. When Colette was surveying the scene in Paris, just before the outbreak of war, she wrote in a newspaper article of the feverish craze for the tango and described how one woman had danced herself to death from peritonitis: 'She finally confessed that for two and a half months, and almost without noticing it, she had danced the tango for seven, eight and sometimes eleven hours a day, always wearing fairly tight shoes with high heels.' In 1910, 'in an automobile heading towards Marseilles', André Gide had had time to note in his diary

that 'locating the idea of perfection, not in equilibrium and the middle path but in the extreme and exaggeration is perhaps what will most set off our period and distinguish it most annoyingly'. The *haute couture* designer Jean Worth, head of one of the longest-lived *couture* houses in Paris, felt that by 1914 popular fashion had become 'one meaningless jangle hopelessly out of tune'. He noted sadly that former standards in dress were being abandoned, that the 'sweet reasonableness' of the previous generation was forgotten. He considered: 'It seems to synchronize with the growing restlessness of this age, an age of fast motors and flying machines and feverish craze for excitement and distraction.'

The pace of life in the world of the Fine Arts was no less feverish, and it is an important factor when considering the origins of the new impetus in fashion illustration. The need was there, for a more inventive approach, and the Fine Arts provided much of the fresh imagery on which the illustrators could draw. In a sense it can be seen that the work of Georges Lepape, Paul Iribe, George Barbier and the other young illustrators filtered and slightly mellowed the work of the avant-garde in the other arts. During the first years of these young illustrators' professional lives, art events had taken place in Paris which must have been enormously exciting for them, events which are now of historic importance. Matisse and his

Above: This deft and pretty picture was painted by André Marty, for *Modes et Manières d'Aujourd'hui* of 1919, published in 1921. It not only shows the rich lining of the cape and the fashionable silhouette beneath but also includes a complex skyscape in which graceful flights of duck contrast with a biplane chugging in the opposite direction

Far left: Georges Barbier captured the new, sharper outline of women's dress in his illustration for the *Journal des Dames et des Modes* in April 1914, and echoed it in his composition. Typically, he also included the seeds of a story in the chance offer of shelter beneath an umbrella

friends exhibited new paintings at the *Salon d'Automne* in October 1905, shocking the public enough into calling them 'Wild Beasts' or *Fauves*, yet these initially unpalatable images and styles with their loose brush strokes and bright colours, were absorbed by the fashion illustrators and came out in their work in a more socially acceptable form.

The Futurists, in their activist manifesto of 1910, glorifying war, speed and machines, threw yet more criticism at established views on art, and also produced a document bemoaning the banality of the conventional approach to clothing and advocating as a cure, their 'hap-hap-hap-hap-happy clothes'. Equally provocative but more acceptable, perhaps because it took place safely within a theatre, was the arrival, with the Russian Ballet, of Bakst's extraordinarily inventive costume and set designs which introduced brilliant colour combinations and fluid, exotic uses of fabric. The Cubists too, before the war, were contributing to the rearrangement of the old order of art, and Picasso, in exploring new avenues in painting, had been greatly attracted by African sculpture. Non-European art forms had attracted a number of painters before him: Van Gogh, Gauguin and Bernard had been intrigued by Japanese prints at the end of the nineteenth century, and exhibitions of these prints had been staged in Paris in the 1880s and 1890s. The young fashion illustrators were obviously influenced by Japanese prints too, and even whilst Georges Lepape, for

Above: One of Janine Aghian's most charming and decorative pages done for *The Essence of the Mode of the Day*, published in 1920. It shows just how high the standards of illustration were in the limited edition albums and fashion magazines. The rich colours and finely elongated human figures are as fresh and new as any to be found in more serious easel painting

Right: Afternoon clothes illustrated for the *Gazette du Bon Ton*, May 1920, by Robert Bonfils. The style of painting retains certain features typical of the pre-1914 style, such as the foliage, and solid areas of colour. In keeping with the *Gazette*'s confident reappearance after the war, however, the artist has introduced a brisk, sketchy style of drawing and new acid colours, elements which came to dominate the illustrations of the 1920s

18

example, was a student at the École des Beaux-Arts, an exhibition of seventeenth and eighteenth century prints from Japan was held there in 1902. Any young artist interested in these prints would have had no difficulty in finding them in Paris before the war; large exhibitions of them were held annually from 1909 to 1914 at the Musée des Arts Décoratifs and in 1905 Migeon published his important book *Chefs d'Oeuvre d'art Japonais*.

New energy in the visual arts and some of these non-European influences combined with a feeling in pre-1914 France that something different in fashion illustration was required to match not only the mood of the new fashions but also the more venturesome social climate which many people had openly recognized. The two albums commissioned by Paul Poiret from Iribe and Lepape, in 1908 and 1911 respectively, demonstrate most vividly and concisely what crystallized from that pre-1914 situation and then set the tone for the post-war fashion illustrations. Both picture albums benefitted enormously from being illustrated solely by one artist and from being commissioned by a patron, Poiret, who did not have his eye only on the world of *haute couture* but who was in touch with many of the arts of his time – for example, he had his own portrait painted by Derain.

What Iribe did in the first album, *Les Robes de Paul Poiret*, in

Below: *The Water Chute* by Charles Martin, from *Sports et Divertissements*, dated 1914, but not published until 1920. Martin was particularly fond of and very successful with more modernist styles which were finding their way into fashion illustration and decorative albums

1908, was to banish many of the traditional ingredients of fashion illustration and leave the mannequins boldly grouped on a clear white ground, with only a few other items inked in, in a brief, brisk style, just to set the scene, whether indoors or out. When Lepape was given the limelight by Poiret in 1911, he produced a similar sized album called *Les Choses de Paul Poiret vues par Georges Lepape* but in a style which finally showed that fashion illustration had, without doubt, come of age. The very fact that Poiret published his *couture* collection 'as seen' by Lepape indicates the improved status of illustrators generally.

From the Japanese prints Lepape and other illustrators learned to array curvilinear figures against a rectilinear, often grid-like, background, or to give the picture's surface the appearance of a tilt or twist or an airy height with the minimum of brush work, often achieving this new liveliness by dispensing with a middle ground entirely. In their compositions the foreground was often tilted upwards, the middle ground thus disappeared and the background became a backdrop, in the theatrical sense. These young fashion illustrators injected the life and movement so much needed in their art at that time by adjusting the onlooker's apparent angle with the flat picture plane and his distance from it, all tricks known to painters but hitherto unexploited fully in fashion illustration.

Below: An example of the increasing complexity of styles both in fashion and in decorative illustration. By André Marty, for the 1919 edition of *Modes et Manières d'Aujourd'hui*, which was published in 1921

From the adventurous palettes of the *Fauves* and the stronger range of colours in *haute couture*, the illustrators took courage and began to introduce previously unused degrees of brightness and contrast. From the Cubists came yet more new interpretations of mass and space. Lepape's painting of the single turbaned head in 1911, in *Les Choses de Paul Poiret*, shows very clearly indeed this new spatial arrangement, the fresh experiments with colour and the enterprising treatment of the human face. With only four strokes for the nose and mouth, Lepape gave the model's face all the pouting, sultry exoticism Poiret could have wished for, capturing all the fascination Poiret himself felt for the bejewelled turbans he had first seen in the Victoria and Albert Museum in London and which had set him off on a whole range of turban designs for fashionable women. No doubt Lepape and his contemporaries had seen some of Modigliani's novel visions of the human face in his paintings in Paris and had spotted how they too could take up and use in their own illustrations the compellingly vacant eyes he often painted. Another source for this sudden revision of the images of women in fashion illustration may well have been the early silent movies. Some of the faces which gaze at us from the pre-1914 fashion plates are very like the pale faces of the girls who flickered across the screen in those days, with heavy eye make-up and uncertain lighting effects combining to make their darkened eyes eerie against their unnaturally white skins, and the exact outline of their cheeks or noses hard to distinguish.

The fashion illustrators in France at this time also had the added advantage of renewed interest in the *pochoir* printing process which was particularly well suited to their style of work and by which a great proportion of it was reproduced. In France this printing technique had had a long history. It is known, for example, that it was used by the card manufacturers of Lyons in the fifteenth century. In those days the *pochoir* itself, which simply means the stencil, would have been of oiled pasteboard, but the method perfected in France in the early twentieth century used a zinc or bronze stencil. These stencils, when skilfully employed, could build up each colour and finally reproduce all the shades of the original to an almost infinite complexity. Jean Saudé, one of the best exponents of this printing method, wrote of using over thirty different stencils to reproduce the freshness of a delicate water-colour. The stencils could also be used to colour in pre-printed

Left: Illustration by André Marty, for the *Gazette du Bon Ton*, July 1922. The mirror was often used by illustrators as it gave them a chance to show both front and back of the garment in the same painting. Poiret designed this evening costume in the less flamboyant style which was typical of his work from the end of the First World War until he closed his design house altogether, but it retains the elaborate embroidery for which his house was so renowned

Right: This page by Anni Offterdinger appeared in the March 1923 edition of the German magazine *Styl*. The outrageously elongated figures and brisk drawing techniques, combined with subtle colour contrasts, were important elements in the vigorous and zany style of illustration so characteristic of the better fashion periodicals of the 1920s

outlines either of particular figures or of the entire design.

In comparison with photographic or other entirely mechanical means of reproduction, the *pochoir* method is slow and laborious. Yet, for this very reason it enjoyed its vogue with Saudé and Vogel and other publishers aiming for very high quality reproduction. The *pochoir* method, being manual rather than mechanical and building up a design layer by layer, was able at all its stages to retain the virtues of handwork and thereby copy and convey an image remarkably faithful to the spirit of the original – an advantage which modern silk-screen printing shares. This factor made *pochoir* printing eminently suitable for the *de luxe* books and fashion periodicals so beloved in France at that time, and during those years the process was perfected to the highest standards.

Although less known and little used elsewhere, its obvious advantages were much admired by connoisseurs of printing and in 1930, in the annual English review of international graphics, *The Penrose Annual*, D. B. Bliss wrote that 'the freshness and elegance inherent in the process is readily felt but hard to analyse'. It is regrettable that he was to prove somewhat over-optimistic in noting that 'there is little doubt that there is a great future for it in this country'. Somehow there never was to the same extent outside France, for France was always more willing to experiment with, and enjoy, very limited editions of books of high quality printing and illustration.

The group of illustrators who collectively were responsible for injecting the new life into the fashion illustrations of the period up to 1939, and for providing some of the very tenacious influences on the fashion photographers who followed them, were conscious of being a group, friendly and close to each other, especially the seven who became Lucien Vogel's main team for his famed *Gazette du Bon Ton*. One reason for their sense of brotherhood was that most of them were trained at the great Parisian art school, the École des Beaux-Arts. Vogel's original group comprised George Barbier, Paul Iribe, Georges Lepape, Charles Martin, André Marty, Bernard Boutet de Monvel, and also Pierre Brissaud. Together they were later remembered as the 'Knights of the Bracelet', for they wore bracelets, as part of their fastidiously stylish and immaculate image. They were certainly never keen to appear as starving artists in cold garrets, however few the outlets for their sort of illustration may have been when they set out to

Right: These designs by Beer and Patou were painted by Bacly for the January 1924 edition of *Art, Goût, Beauté*. It shows how widespread was the taste at that time for the geometric designs in contrasting colours to be found in furniture fabric, ceramics, or any item of the applied arts

Below: Men's sporting wear, designed by George Harrison and painted by Benito for *L'Homme Élégant*, November 1920. Benito's slightly metallic style was often characterized by sharply elongated figures and a love for gleaming motorcars

Art - Goût - Beauté

27

Right: For a 1924 issue of the *Gazette du Bon Ton*, its penultimate year, Georges Lepape painted Jeanne Lanvin's designs of dresses for a bride and bridesmaid. Exquisitely intricate workmanship continued in the workrooms of the Paris *couture* houses, and the illustrator painted it appreciatively

make their livings. René Gimpel, the art dealer and patron, recorded a visit to Georges Lepape's apartment in the rue Notre Dame de Lorette in Paris in 1918, by which time he considered Lepape to be one of the leaders of the modern decorative arts movement, noting carefully the violet-coloured wallpaper and silver cushions he saw there.

Apart from fashion illustration in the *Gazette* and magazines such as *Luxe de Paris, Art, Goût, Beauté* or *Le Jardin des Modes*, these artists also illustrated the many luxury and limited edition books produced at the time. Brissaud for example illustrated *Eugénie Grandet* in 1913 and George Barbier the beautiful *Danses de Nejinski* and *Les Chansons de Bilitis*. Others, like Bernard Boutet de Monvel, also exhibited paintings at the Paris Salons; Lepape designed ballet costumes; Marty wrote reviews of modern dance; and Iribe designed furniture.

With this wealth of talent and the renewed interest in the *pochoir* method, it is not surprising that a whole host of limited-edition magazines sprang up: *Modes et Manières d'Aujourd'hui, Journal des Dames et des Modes,* and *Gazette du Bon Ton* in 1912, *La Guirlande des Mois* in 1917, *Art, Goût, Beauté* in 1922 and *Falbalas et Fanfreluches* in 1920, and many other magazines, folders and periodicals. Of these the *Gazette du Bon Ton* always managed to convey the quality of a carefully compiled book; it carried as much text as illustration and both parts sustained equally high standards and a coherent style. Even now, though sometimes well-thumbed and a little tatty, its pages retain great charm and wit. After the last issue of this excellent magazine in 1925, nothing else quite like it was ever produced. It had the prestige of having pioneered the idea of using the very best artists to illustrate the very best *haute couture* designs, of having maintained a superb standard of printing on hand-made paper, and for most of its life it was guided by one director, Lucien Vogel. Although it always had contemporaries and competitors, the *Gazette* was probably the most consistently good at its job, and could be said to be the best of a very good bunch. Its illustrations reproduced in this book, together with those from *Journal des Dames et des Modes, Modes et Manières d'Aujourd'hui, Feuillets d'Art* and many others, will convey to the newcomer some of the attraction of these increasingly rare publications, and will be a welcome sight to those already familiar with them. With the aid of these illustrations from his private collection, and extracts from the editorials, Julian Robinson evokes, in the pages that follow, the fashionable world in which these magazines flourished and captures the visual excellence of this creative period.

The Age of Opulence
1901-1911

If, early one sunny morning, during the first decade of the century, you had found yourself by chance in the open space of the Place de l'Opéra you would have seen a crowd of many thousands, advancing from all directions, to the rue Auber, rue Halévy, rue de la Paix and the Place Vendôme. There in the small, dingy workshops of the *Grands Couturiers*, this army of seamstresses, beaders, embroideresses, tailors, fitters, cutters, milliners and furriers contrived to make the elaborate, decorated gowns then in fashion.

For the fashionable rich, this was the flamboyant era known as the *Belle Époque*, when *Art Nouveau* was at its height. Inspired by the free-flowing shapes and restless, swirling, rhythmic curves of this design style, the *Grands Couturiers* of the day, who dressed the fashionable women of the world, used to the full yards and yards of luxurious materials in their dresses and gowns – flowing flounces of pleated *chiffon*, the finest silk satins embellished with colourful embroidery, *lamés* and *Jacquard* fabrics enriched with beadwork,

Left: Dress photographed by Reutlinger in August 1901, for *Les Modes*. The skirt train has been carefully draped towards the camera to show its intricate and luxurious quality. The bodice also displays the variety of skilled workmanship offered by the *couturiers* to their clients. Stiffly posed in a formal setting, this photograph has utilized the same features as contemporary engraved fashion illustration

layers of hand-tucking and ruching, and yards and yards of the finest lace edgings.

During this opulent and extravagant period, an elegant woman would visit the *haute couture* houses of Paris not only to discover what the new fashionable styles were to be, but also to be seen there by her best friends – as well as by her best enemies. If she was a woman of the world from the social *élite* of New York or London, Paris, St Petersburg, Berlin or Buenos Aires she would come in late February or March to choose her spring and summer clothes, and in late August or September for those to wear that autumn and winter.

Here with the help of her *vendeuse*, one of the *couturier's* team of saleswomen with whom she always dealt and who knew all her personal and financial secrets, she would choose her wardrobe for the next six months: *peignoirs* and *lingeries*, simple costumes for the morning errands and more ornate ones for morning visits, luncheon frocks, afternoon gowns and walking dresses, gowns for visiting and those to be worn when receiving visitors. And finally, an endless list of gowns for special occasions which must never be left to chance: gowns for family gatherings, for official ceremonies, for lectures and sermons; grander ones for first nights and artistic receptions; gowns for dinner parties, concerts or balls; others for a supper at the cabaret, and yet another for the theatre; not to mention the races, visits out of town, motor-car trips, train journeys,

Below: Summer dresses photographed by Boyer in June 1901, for the magazine *Les Modes*, showing the fashionable female silhouette of the *Belle Époque*, the bodices loaded with frills and flounces, a small constricted waist, and ground length skirts filled out by pleats and extra fabric to form a full train at the rear

sea voyages and visits to the seaside and the mountains – an endless selection, the sole purpose of which seems to have been the avoidance of speculation by one's friends or criticism by one's enemies.

On looking through the fashionable magazines of that period, it is possible to study the designs of such *Grands Couturiers* as Worth, Redfern, Paquin, Doeuillet, Doucet and the Callot Soeurs from the hand-coloured engravings which depicted every seam and flounce, button and bow, in minute if static and uninspired detail. For although *Art Nouveau* was at its height, no hint of its free-flowing style was to be seen in fashion illustration. During the latter half of the nineteenth century numerous experiments had taken place in Europe and the United States of America to replace these traditional fashion plates, which had dominated the world of high fashion for 120 years, by using industrialized methods, such as chromo-lithography and mechanically-reproduced photographs.

Left: Women motoring in Paris in 1901. Fashionable women considered it necessary to have different sets of garments for different occasions, during the *Belle Époque*. The requirement was not merely for day or evening wear, but also for town and country, dancing, lunching and even motoring

Right: A group of mannequins display the 1909 autumn collection of the Doucet *couture* house. By that year waistlines were much higher. Several dresses in this group have features which accentuate the freer, more elongated silhouette which was being so forcefully promoted at this time such as a long sash falling to the ground or an asymmetric embroidered motif which goes from the bust to the floor

Below: Three ladies being helped by their *vendeuse* to make their selection from the winter collection of the Martial et Armand *couture* house in Paris. Everything about this scene conveys a sense of comfortable spaciousness, and long afternoons with nothing to do but choose from the wide range of luxury handmade clothes

Right: 1909, a lady and an assistant settle down to the pleasures of selecting and decorating a stylishly large hat from the befeathered and beribboned collection available at the Paquin *couture* house millinery rooms

But it was not until 1901 that a way of reproducing photographs was perfected which had the same look of fashionable quality.

It was not long before a completely new style of high-quality fashion magazine appeared to replace those 'appalling fashion plate monstrosities' using this newly developed coloured photographic method of illustration. Although many of the previously influential fashion plate magazines were to continue in circulation, within a very short time these new magazines became the showplace for all the very best in fashion and the decorative arts.

The most influential of these high-quality magazines was *Les Modes*, which was published in France for sale in Paris, London, Berlin and New York. The format was larger than most of its established competitors, measuring 11 inches by 14 inches as against the previously fashionable *Journal des Demoiselles*' 8 inches by 11 inches. *Les Modes* featured *haute couture* dresses, furniture, jewellery and many other aspects of the decorative and applied arts of the period, using half-tone photographs printed on high-quality glossy paper with a number of additional tipped-in pages of coloured photographs, with tremendous success. All the *couturiers* sought to have their dresses photographed and coloured by such leading society photographers as Mlle Reutlinger and Paul Nadar for *Les Modes*, and in the first few issues designs by Redfern, Paquin, Doeuillet, Doucet, and La Ferrière were included. Photographs of the latest jewellery designs by Vever, Lalique and Maugeant were also featured, as was furniture by Gaillard, de Feure and Aubert, light fittings by Dampt and glass by Gallé, together with numerous other decorative items. For the first time the fashionable societies of the major cultural centres of the world could see what the latest designs actually looked like, and not the engraver's interpretation of them – the innovation of coloured

Below: At the Cheruit *couture* house in 1910 fitters work on a client's new spring dress. The waist is high and the front far smoother and more closely fitted than it would have been a few years before, but this client has chosen to keep a long, full train

photographs of design styles as they actually existed out-dated that influence almost overnight.

With the new method of illustration came a new style of editorial which was as revolutionary in its effect as were the pictures against which it competed. This journalistic influence is most strongly seen in the American magazines of that period, such as *Vogue* and *Harper's Bazar*, which used half-tone and line illustrations with evocative 'word pictures' to convey the latest fashion news instead of the newly-introduced coloured photographs of the French magazine *Les Modes*.

During the next few years most of the European quality magazines promoted the whole field of fashion and the decorative arts, giving as much weight to reporting the latest creations of Paquin, Doucet or the Callot Soeurs as to the latest styles in *Art Nouveau* furniture, jewellery or interior designs. Later, in the Great War both *Vogue* and *Harper's Bazar* would use evocative captions to focus on a variety of different items featured in the same edition, such as 'The time has come, designers say, to talk of many things, of shoes and furs and lingerie and if one flares or clings, and where the waistline ought to be and whether hats have wings' or in a less poetic vein 'When is a lampshade not a lampshade? When it is a hat . . . in blue cloth with woolly flowers growing on it and worsted tassels hanging down.'

In 1902 an exhibition was held in Turin of the best examples of the current decorative arts, with important *Art Nouveau* exhibits coming from Scotland, Austria, France, Italy and Germany. For the first time in over twenty years there was a challenge to the more flowery aspects of the style which had during the latter part of the nineteenth century succumbed to the seductive opulence of the *Belle Époque*. This challenge was mainly seen in the clear-cut simplicity of Josef Hoffmann from Vienna, in the Celtic influence shown in the elongated, black or stark white furniture by Mackintosh and MacNairn from the Glasgow School, and in the work of the Italian designer Carlo Bugatti, all of whom exhibited a visual hostility to much of the luxuriant showiness of the more opulent aspects of the currently fashionable styles.

By the middle of the first decade of the century, the new technology – exemplified in the most recent automobile – was having an effect in determining, for example, that the fashion conscious

Below: Behind the luxurious collections of Parisian *haute couture* were dozens of highly skilled workers. Each designer had his own workshops such as this one in which the girls labour over their frames, beading and embroidering precious fabrics

Right: A page from Paul Iribe's 1908 album, *Les Robes de Paul Poiret*. In spite of the traditional 'props' such as the painting and the chair, which the more cautious illustrators had always used, this was a very adventurous experiment in fashion illustration. Large areas show the bare colour of the handmade paper, one mannequin has been turned away from us, the face of the other has been drawn in with minimal pen strokes, and in the coloured areas there is no shading. The success of this album led to the adoption of these features by many of the best of the young fashion illustrators

should all dress in preparation for a 'short spin'. Some of the prettiest coats for autumn were *manteaux automobiles*, cut straight from the shoulder to about fifteen inches below the waist. These short autumn coats were worn with those 'amazing short skirts' of 1906 which scarcely reached to the ankle.

At the same time a new young Paris *couturier*, Paul Poiret, was beginning to catch the headlines. He had opened his small *salon* at 5 rue Auber in September 1903, after working for both Doucet and Worth, and by the autumn of 1906 he had begun to develop a more fluid style of dress which fell in a straight tubular manner from the bust, without the need for corsets or restrictive petticoats. Two years later his novel designs were published in a beautifully printed album, *Les Robes de Paul Poiret*, with illustrations by Paul Iribe – a masterly set of ink drawings coloured by the *pochoir* process of hand stencilling developed by Jean Saudé. In this revolutionary album, Iribe juxtaposed traditional line drawing with blocks of flat unshaded colour on the dresses themselves, playing down such background 'props' as a table, a sofa or a balustrade to maximize the impact of the brilliantly coloured, boldly grouped figures. Iribe's idiosyncratic treatment of Poiret's designs marked the beginning of a new era, not only in fashion but in its illustration too, heralding the birth of the style which is known today as *Art Déco*.

The year of 1908 also witnessed the first invasion into Europe by the Russian Ballet, which underlined the changing aesthetic taste of the Parisian – though in London and New York the audiences were still being entranced by the free-flowing dance created by Isadora Duncan and her followers during the height of the *Art Nouveau* period. It was one year later, however, before Diaghilev's *Ballets Russes* were to capture the artistic heart of Paris, and 1910 before their hearts were set completely alight by the spectacular production of the ballet *Scheherazade*. This ballet, specially commissioned by Serge Diaghilev, introduced the full splendour of oriental design to western Europe. The influence of such a riot of colour, such a mountain of cushions, such enormous golden lamps, such bejewelled costumes, was immense and its impact on fashion and the decorative arts far reaching. For the fashion designer, Bakst's sumptuous costumes and exotic sets meant still more. With his talent for using fabric in such a way as to suggest great luxury and yet leave the dancer free and unimpeded, Bakst demonstrated beyond doubt that mobility and luxury were not necessarily incompatible, thereby sowing the seeds, as Poiret was also doing, of an entirely new attitude towards dress.

PAUL IRIBE

Art Déco Revolution
1911-1919

Twice a year, in February and in August, the *salons* of the *Grands Couturiers* were thrown open to the designers and buyers from throughout Europe, the United States and South America, who came to buy models to copy, to take stock of the current tastes and to question the 'Oracle of Fashion'.

Even for the most jaded eyes, those collections of 1911 must have been a dazzling spectacle, for after hesitating at the cross-roads of fashion since the arrival of the *Ballets Russes*, the most influential of the French *haute couturiers* plunged boldly down a new thoroughfare clearly marked '*To Mecca*'. Had those Paris *couturiers* really designed all these orientally-inspired dresses themselves, or had they rubbed one of those beautiful lamps from *Scheherezade* to invoke some wondrous *djin* and conjured him to make them? For fashions at some of the *Grandes Maisons* of 1911 certainly seemed the work of oriental wizardry which could only have been inspired by eastern magic.

Far left: Charles Martin's illustration of a design for a fanciful dress by Redfern, which appeared in the *Gazette du Bon Ton* in February 1913. For sheer panache, luxury, and colourfulness the *Gazette*'s illustrations had few rivals. Charles Martin was one of the original group of artists whose work launched this magazine

Above: A page from Georges Lepape's 1911 album of illustrations, *Les Choses de Paul Poiret*, showing the turbans Poiret was then producing

Left: A firework display depicted by Georges Lepape from *Les Choses de Paul Poiret*. Lepape extended some of Iribe's design features, treating the whole page with flat areas of colour, and making it a coherent scene in its own right. The chequered floor became a favourite device of fashion illustrators, and, later, of photographers. It was a means of emphasizing the raised, theatrical sensation and disposing of the middle ground

After the parade of the collection, the materials were studied: exotic fabrics, designed under the influence of Bakst, in heavy silk brocades and *brocatelles* flecked with gold, silver and steel or embroidered with fantastic designs in the vivid colours normally reserved for the stage effects contrived for Diaghilev.

At the centre of this whirlwind of change was Paul Poiret, with his newly designed spring collection and his well-timed publication of the second luxury album of his designs, illustrated by the almost unknown Georges Lepape. Poiret gave the same wide scope to this second protégé, and Lepape made the album, *Les Choses de Paul Poiret*, an exquisite tribute. He followed Iribe's example of using bold areas of flat colours but removed all vestiges of the traditional line-drawn background leaving much of the page in some designs entirely white and empty, while his use of the dropped eye-level, to make the observer feel as if he were peering up at a raised stage, and his habit of drawing models with their backs to the viewer to given an air of mystery, became stock-in-trade for illustrators

as well as fashion photographers right through to the 1930s. Lepape's designs at last gave fashion illustration a fully-fledged style of its own and in doing so, not only did he display Poiret's designs to a wider public but launched his own career too. From then on, in his own field, he was to be as much in demand as his patron, Paul Poiret, was in his.

Being a grand showman with a perfect sense of timing, Poiret gave a spectacular summer party as a 'Persian Celebration' to publicize the oriental fashions he had launched five months earlier with *Les Choses de Paul Poiret* and wished to repeat in the autumn. He invited three hundred guests to come to this 'One Thousand and Second Night', dressed as ancient Persians, reserving of course the position of Sultan for himself. He was dressed in a pale grey quilted caftan edged in fur and belted with green silk. He wore a pair of ruby-red velvet buskins which were decorated with gold filigree, on his head was a white, bejewelled silk turban, and he carried a short sabre and an ivory-handled whip as a symbol of his authority. To complete the regal effect, Poiret sat in splendour on an elaborately decorated throne next to his personal 'imperial gold cage of beautiful favourites and exotic slaves'.

In the grounds of his eighteenth-century mansion in the Avenue d'Antin, pink ibis, white peacocks and flamingoes wandered, whilst parrots, macaws and monkeys were chained to the trees which were

Above left: An illustration painted by Paul Iribe in 1911 for a luxury album, or catalogue, of *haute couture* designs, for the house of Paquin. Inspired to colour the sky a glowing yellow and the sea a deep green, Iribe perfectly complemented the rich blue of the model's dress. The urn of tumbling flowers, the dangerous angle of the balustrade and the tree painted in Japanese style all add up to a floating world of rapture, an abandonment of reason and a love of sensuality undreamt of by the previous generation of fashion illustrators

Right: This is a page by Georges Lepape, done for a 1912 edition of *Les modes et Manières d'Aujourd'hui*. The scene depicts a little story as well as showing the dress off to effect. An outrageously green lawn and an entirely empty background convey the simple joys of a butterfly chase more convincingly than the elaborately worked and overcrowded engravings of earlier fashion illustrators could ever have done

Above: Georges Lepape illustrated this page of the 1912 *Modes et Manières d'Aujourd'hui*, using a palette of so-called 'unrealistic' colours. He was no doubt encouraged by the colours in the Fauvist and other avant-garde paintings

Above right: Another page by Georges Lepape for the 1912 *Modes et Manières d'Aujourd'hui*. The skirt and overblouse are remarkable not only for the gay brightness of the colours but for the loose cut resulting in a very free silhouette. Such clothes were reserved for country wear only

Right: This banquet scene from the 1912 *Modes et Manières d'Aujourd'hui*, by Georges Lepape, shows the more constricting but exotic styles for evening wear, and the turban which Paul Poiret was popularizing so successfully

scattered with coloured lights. In the courtyard there was·a gargantuan buffet under a painted awning by Raoul Dufy, and in a recreated 'Old Persian Market' slave traders, fortune tellers, marmoset merchants, beggars, tailors, cobblers and sweetmeat sellers plied their wares. There were numerous Eastern cooks preparing exotic dishes which were served with strangely spiced drinks. Flutes and zithers played as the guests reclined on large, colourful cushions and soft rugs to watch Persian entertainers and exotic *divertissements*, whilst a slim white nude slave danced under a cloud of gauze. At the height of the evening's entertainment the Sultan's 'imperial gold cage of beautiful favourites' was flung open and out stepped Madame Poiret, wearing Paul Poiret's latest creation of loosely-cut harem pantaloons in white and ochre *chiffon*, fitting tightly at the waist and ankles, under a short hooped tunic of gauzy gold *lamé* which swayed in the summer breeze like some exotic eastern flower. The bodice was of *chiffon* and gold *lamé* held in with a wide cummerbund, and the wide sleeves were edged with fur. A gold *lamé* Persian turban with a tall aigrette plume fastened with a turquoise clip completed this exquisite outfit.

The success of this publicity spectacular was immense, and the continuing success of the Paul Poiret 'Oriental Collections' was

Left: Charles Martin on this page of the 1913 *Modes et Manières d'Aujourd'hui* added a touch of nocturnal magic by encircling the model's head with fireflies

Right: Page for the 1913 *Modes et Manières d'Aujourd'hui*. Charles Martin has placed the figure behind the table and the trellis, showing an increasing interest in composition and the balance of colours for their own sake

assured when it was reported that in the following few days his *salon* was filled with most of the fashionable ladies of Paris ordering copies of his 'lampshade tunic' and 'harem pantaloons'. Although some critics and rival *couturiers* described his new fashion as 'vulgar, wicked and ugly', his revolutionary harem pantaloons had finally freed the fashionable legs of the world from the shackles of the tight 'hobble, toddle, toil and wobble' gown of the later part of the *Belle Époque*. In retrospect it is possible to see that the Parisians had been flirting with orientalia since the beginning of the century with exhibitions and imported novelties but it took the impact of Diaghilev's *Ballets Russes* and the flair of Paul Poiret to seize the mood of change and lift it to magnificent beauty.

During the summer months of 1911, when the flowers were at

Left: Outfits for St Moritz, painted by George Barbier. This page appeared in the *Journal des Dames et des Modes* in February 1913. The practical suit of warm wool edged with fur has an added touch of luxury in the embroidered panel and lapel. Barbier's work at this point had a characteristically brief, concise style

Above right: An outfit especially designed for going to the races, illustrated in 1913 by J. van Brock for the July edition of the *Journal des Dames et des Modes*. The layered skirt reveals the whole foot, and anticipates the raised hemlines which appeared during the First World War

Below right: George Barbier often used black backgrounds in his illustrations of luxury evening wear. This background depicts a Japanese screen and emphasizes the Japanese-style silhouette which so many evening clothes echoed at this time. The coat and dress copy a kimono's shape with multi-layered, sloping shoulders, overloading the torso and cascading down to a narrow hemline which enforced a delicate and mincing gait. From the *Journal des Dames et des Modes*, October 1913

their best, the fashionable women of London, Paris and New York were to be seen in enormous hats decorated with flowers trimmed with ribbons, ruched fabrics, braids, lace, feathers and furs, together with buttons, buckles, medallions, embroidery, pearls and colourful gems. For the winter season fur was decidedly the most handsome and distinguished trimming, with opossum, Canadian fox and musquash being reserved for the newly fashionable tailor-mades, whilst elegant velvets and plush dress-maker garments were completed with skunk and the costly chinchilla. For the enthusiastic lady motorist there were warm reversible coats in woollen materials, others were of soft leather with a brightly coloured cloth lining, whilst still others were in traditional plain English material, combined with fox or skunk and lined in squirrel in its natural grey or dyed as imitation mink. The evening dresses – always the most fanciful and capricious items in a lady's *toilette* – were made in the finest lace and dainty tulle, threaded either with straw paillettes, large paste motifs or irisating beaded rays . . . figured *crêpe de Chine*, soft silk *crépon* in rose and orange tints with veilings in tone . . . smooth satin in glowing colours . . . soft muslins and clinging shaded velvet.

During that winter and the following spring, the American musical invasion was at its height, Tin Pan Alley supplying most of the latest novelty music sheets and American phonograph records providing most of the latest popular recorded music. The big break-through for American popular music had come several years earlier with the Negro-inspired Cake Walk and then the Turkey Trot with Elsie Janice, the queen of those new-style popular dances, until the newly-married Castles arrived in Paris. Vernon and Irene Castle, who were destined to have a fantastic success throughout Europe and America dancing their interpretation of 'the immodest tango' and the 'daring fox trot', created as big a sensation at the Café de Paris as Nijinsky was destined to make when dancing *L'Après-midi d'un Faune* the following year.

In 1912 the first issue of *Modes et Manières d'Aujourd'hui* was published by Pierre Corrard, containing twelve stylish illustrations in colour by Georges Lepape. This was the first of a series of seven special *de luxe* hand-printed albums of designs in the newly introduced *Art Déco* style which had been so successful in *Les Choses de Paul Poiret*. As with the earlier album, the method of printing was the hand-stencilled *pochoir* method, in which each of the twelve illustrations went through thirty different hand-colouring processes using *gouache* paint which exactly matched the artist's original. The

Right: This afternoon dress was designed by Martial and Armand, and appeared in *Luxe de Paris* in June 1913. A practical garment, it was made for a gentle stroll

Below: Painting of a Doucet dress by Leonnel, in *Luxe de Paris*, May 1913

Far right: Another witty composition by George Barbier for the 1914 album, *Modes et Manières d'Aujourd'hui*. The long train of the dress and the draped ropes of pearls make an elegant silhouette, but such clothes confined the lady's movements almost as much as the cage confined the bird she has just released

limited edition of three hundred copies was printed on the finest Imperial *Japon* paper by Jean Saudé, who had developed the *pochoir* process. Each *de luxe* copy was signed and numbered by the artist and the printer.

The following month, in June 1912, the first of the seventy-nine issues of the *Journal des Dames et des Modes* was published by Vaugirard of Paris, with Jacques de Nouvion as *directeur*. This small, influential journal contained illustrations by most of the leading artists of the day, including George Barbier, Brunelleschi, Iribe, Van Brock, Vallée, Valentin Gross and Bakst, all printed by the *pochoir* process.

Towards the end of 1912 the most famous of all these new-style magazines was published. Its name was the *Gazette du Bon Ton*, and it was published by the Librairie Centrale des Beaux-Arts, with Lucien Vogel as *directeur*. To ensure that each issue of this limited edition *de luxe* magazine would feature only the very best

Left: Page from the *Gazette du Bon Ton*, of May 1913 showing a Doeuillet dress painted by André Marty. Like his fellow *Gazette* illustrators, Marty at this time favoured the use of a pun or witticism to emphasize the mood of a dress, in addition to a carefully designed composition which in this case contrasts the delicacy and vulnerability of the *robe de lingerie* against a dark landscape

Right: For the 1914 *Modes et Manières d'Aujourd'hui*, George Barbier painted this boating scene in the clear, light style he had developed. By 1914 the hemline was beginning to creep upwards, and this dress for a boating trip is not only pretty but is a practical length, revealing the ankles. At the end of the nineteenth century, there had been much debate as to how a lady's dress could combine feminine beauty with utility. The gradual evolution of fashion towards that dual achievement was accelerated during the First World War

of the newest design ideas and the most fashionable novelties, Lucien Vogel enlisted the co-operation of the leading Paris *couturiers* of the period – Cheruit, Doeuillet, Paquin, Poiret, Redfern and Worth. And using the *pochoir* method of printing, which admirably suited the highly stylized illustrations, he captured for posterity the essence of the new *Art Déco* movement.

As with *Modes et Manières* and *Journal des Dames*, the *Gazette du Bon Ton* was expensive to produce and exclusive in its aim. As was stated at the time, its expensiveness and exclusiveness were essential to its success: it was to be 'a showcase in which only the most luxurious examples of high fashion and the best of the decorative arts could be displayed, regardless of the cost involved'. This policy enabled Lucien Vogel to finance the collaboration

between the best pictorial artists of the time and the great fashion designers of the age, for which the magazine became justly famous. During its fourteen years of intermittent publication *couturiers* such as Beer, Lanvin, Doeuillet, Paquin, Poiret, Redfern, Cheruit, Worth, Vionnet, Doucet, Martial and Armand reserved for its pages their newest and most brilliant creations. The gowns from these great *maisons de couture* were drawn by artists of such talented inspiration and graceful draftsmanship as Boutet de Monvel, Brissaud, Barbier, Benito, Drian, Erté, Lepape, Martin, Marty, Maggie, Romme, Vallée and Bakst, to name but a few. Each of their illustrations was 'created as a beautiful picture of contemporary life with each design being shown in its own appropriate setting'.

As well as between eight and ten *pochoir* plates, each issue also contained thirty pages of text, profusely illustrated with detailed and decorative line drawings. In all of the sixty-nine issues published between 1912 and 1925, the editorials, articles, *pochoir*

Above: Illustration for the June 1914 issue of the *Journal des Dames et des Modes* by George Barbier, in his most exotic style. The dress reveals the leg almost to the knee, but any suggestion of practicality is suppressed by the long train at the back and the garlands of pearls

Above left: The quality of illustration in the *Journal des Dames et des Modes* closely rivalled that of the *Gazette du Bon Ton*, as this page, designed in 1914 by Robert Dammy, shows. The multi-layered, soft fabric of this dress which is drawn up at the front focuses attention on the impending arrival of much shorter skirts

Above right: A page from the *Gazette du Bon Ton,* April 1914, by Bernard Boutet de Monvel, depicting a Worth evening coat in the setting of the *haute couture* house itself. The difference between the increasing practicality of day wear and the more restrictive exotic evening wear is highlighted in this scene; while the evening dress rests in folds on the floor, the skirts of the *vendeuse* and the client reveal their ankles

illustrations and furniture *croquis*, the format, style and type of paper, were so chosen and combined as to make each issue a joy to look at and handle, and a delight to read, for those fashionable and wealthy members of society who were able to afford, appreciate and interpret its luxurious style. The influence of these three magazines and the style of design they promoted was world-wide; they were sold in London, Paris, New York, Berlin, Geneva, Buenos Aires and St Petersburg.

Another event in that design-busy year of 1912 was Paul Poiret's tour of the major European capitals, complete with his collection of new designs and model girls. He was, by now, not only the most influential *couturier* of the period but also the founder and *directeur* of the influential Martine School of Design, which was grossing three million francs a month for its sales of modern furniture, textiles, murals, wallpapers and decorative items in Paris, London, New York, Berlin and many other major cities. In addition, Poiret had a thriving perfume business, as well as designing for many

Above: One of Georges Lepape's contributions to a special wartime issue of the *Gazette du Bon Ton* celebrating the 'Panama Pacific International Exhibition' of 1915 which was a major event for the beleaguered French *couture* designers trying to expand their export markets. Lepape overcame the wartime economic necessity of placing the designs of seven different designers on the same page by setting them in a naturally crowded scene, a summer afternoon at the fashionable Longchamps racecourse. The dresses show the new phase in fashion, with much wider skirts clearing the ground by several inches

Right: A page designed by George Barbier in 1916 which appeared in the almanac *Guirlande des Mois* the following year. For day wear, skirts got fuller and shorter as the war progressed, and even if fashion illustrators were not called upon to illustrate the war itself, they frequently included references to it, often showing a soldier home on leave as Barbier did here

theatrical productions and co-producing the first fantastic collections of Raoul Dufy fabrics.

The foreign tour of 1912 was an enormous success, as was that of America the following year. These tours had a great influence on the changing design styles of all the decorative arts in the year immediately before the First World War, promoting a wider acceptance of the new *Art Déco* style which combined the luxury of beautiful materials – 'regardless of cost' – with an artistic excellence which no contemporary connoisseur could fail to appreciate. Unfortunately, the term '*Art Déco*' has in recent years been misapplied to the superficially stylized manufactured goods of the 1920s and '30s which would be more correctly described as *kitsch*. The refined luxury of the true *Art Déco* style, which was now being used in all of the most fashionable aspects of the decorative and applied arts, had completely replaced the design influence of the *Art Nouveau* style which had been gradually declining since the end of the *Belle Époque*.

During the following twelve months there were several important exhibitions of contemporary furniture including two in Paris at the *Salon d'Automne* and the *Salon des Arts Décoratifs*. In a leading editorial about these exhibitions, the *Gazette du Bon Ton* said that it was thanks to fashion that the modern design movement had finally succeeded. 'The daring lines of modern clothes, the innovations of style and above all the colours used have opened feminine eyes. Little by little, the vividly-hued cushion has crept, timidly, anxiously, into the *salons* of all the most fashionable houses. And now this intruder has summoned the call to arms. Suddenly the traditional *décor* has aged by several centuries and

Left: Illustration by George Barbier for the *Guirlande des Mois* of 1917. Barbier's inclusion of the long-legged dog echoes not only the more 'leggy' fashions, but also the many references to dogs which were made by wartime fashion journalists who considered the animals to be accessories just as subject to the whims of fashions as the clothes themselves

the air is at last ringing with the hammers of the cabinet-maker, the upholsterer and the decorator.'

The art of book illustration had also been changing during this period of aesthetic resurgence, with the publication of such books as *Le Jardin des Caresses* which was decorated by Leon Carré and printed in *pochoir* by Jean Saudé as a *de luxe* edition of one hundred copies, and *In Powder and Crinoline* with illustrations by Kay Nielsen, printed as a *de luxe* edition of five hundred copies on hand-made paper by Hodder and Stoughton of London. The colour illustrations which were the main attraction of these books were generally reproduced by the newly developed photographic method, using the half-tone colour separation process – although

Above: Georges Lepape painted this impression of the events of August 1914 for the album *Modes et Manières d'Aujourd'hui*, but it did not appear until May 1921

Left: This fantasy on the theme of *Ribbons*, by George Barbier, appeared in the 1918 issue of the *Guirlande des Mois*. It may have been intended as a celebration of the apparently never-ending inventiveness of the Paris fashion designers which had survived the hard days of the First World War

a few of the very expensive French editions were produced with coloured *pochoir* illustrations of the type used in *Modes et Manières* and the *Gazette du Bon Ton*. The style and artistry of these illustrations – not as works of art in the tradition of the great painters, but as beautiful pieces of contemporary design – captured the essence of the period in the illustrators' world of make-believe and fantasy.

In the summer of that fateful year of 1914, the month of June showered gifts upon the fashionable women of London, Paris and New York and among those gifts was a profusion of wonderful *toilettes*. That summer seems to have been a record season for variety with fashions full of wit and fantasy combining both oriental colouring and soft pastel tones. But as the summer season

61

came to an end the mood changed – the French Government decreed a general mobilization and within a few days the holocaust of the First World War had begun.

War or no war, Paris was determined that her role as creator of fashion and arbiter of elegance was not going to be usurped by either London or New York. During the following four years of conflict the *Grands Couturiers* continued as best they could and the export of *haute couture* garments, particularly to the United States, became an important part of the French war effort. The materials of their art may have been in short supply (wool for example could only be obtained once troop requirements had been satisfied) and the nimble fingers of their skilled workers may have been working on munitions, but nevertheless the fashion collections continued to be made.

The Panama Pacific International Exposition held in San Francisco in 1915, far from the guns of Europe, was an ideal venue for the Parisian *couture* houses to demonstrate their pre-eminence in *la mode féminine*. As a special souvenir issue of this exhibition, the *Gazette du Bon Ton* published a joint French and American edition in collaboration with Condé Nast of New York, dated 15th

Above left: A rainy day, by Georges Lepape, for the 1917 *Modes et Manières d'Aujourd'hui*. Lepape's abrupt style harmonized well with the increasing angularity in women's clothes

Above: As well as painting some of the hardships of separation caused by war, Georges Lepape also took delight in the reunions at its end. His more extreme, modernist style begins to become apparent in this 1919 picture of the couple dancing the foxtrot which appeared in the 1921 issue of *Modes et Manières d'Aujourd'hui*

Right: 'Rah-el-Rah', painted by M. Cito for a 1919 issue of the *Guirlande des Mois*. It is one of the last examples of the exotic style of dress and illustration which had been so prevalent in the pre-war period

Above: A version of the layered skirt
painted by George Barbier in 1918, to
appear in the 1919 *Guirlande des Mois*.
Some wartime fashions imitated certain
military features, such as buttoned
pockets or striped cuffs. In this case it is
the hat that has taken on a military
smartness

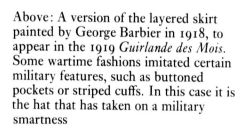

Above right: By Martha Romme, this
advertisement is from a 1919 issue of
Les Feuillets d'Art, a fine periodical
which includes much else besides
fashion. At this time dress designers
were concentrating on the skirt of the
dress. This preoccupation is made clear
in this illustration by layered skirts and
uneven hemlines which anticipate the
major change to much shorter lengths
only a few seasons away

May 1915, as well as a double French edition. The leading article
of the American edition declared that now was the moment for
Paris to express herself according to her custom, and that 'although
a part of French soil is yet in the hands of the invader, Paris remains
as ever the Paris of good taste and fashion', and 'since the Latin
races are fighting to uphold their taste against Teutonic barbarity,
was it not to be expected that Paris Fashion should once again take
the lead this spring?' Sixty new fashions created by the Parisian
Houses were shown within the three major French displays,
entitled 'Vichy', 'Longchamp' and 'The Riviera'; they were
arranged on special wax figures by Pierre Imans against the
beautiful French-inspired background, and drawn with customary
expertise by George Barbier, Étienne Drian and Georges Lepape
for the fashion plates of the *Gazette du Bon Ton*.

The following February, as surely as the first rays of the sun bring
forth a new crop of spring flowers, Paris blossomed in a new selection
of flowered textiles, in colours and patterns nature never intended,
'teasing the colours from the rainbow'. Perhaps in reaction to the

"Fruelider"

Right: A page by Martha Romme from the 1919 *Les Douze Mois de l'Année*, in a style calculated to exaggerate the full skirts and light-headed, zany mood of French fashion just after the First World War

shortages and strain of the harsh wartime conditions, femininity seemed at a premium. It was a magic hour for those manufacturers of silk, *tulle* and lace in France, whose factories and work forces had not been destroyed or depleted by the War. The armed forces had need of stronger fabrics than theirs, and the fashion designers made the best possible use of the more fragile ones.

The major designers realized they must export if they were to survive in business and in the last half of the War, they combined to produce a magazine for circulation abroad called *Les Élégances Parisiennes* which contained a number of illustrations showing each *couture* house's clothes and accessories. It was by no means as attractive a publication as the *Gazette*, for example, had been, but it was as essential for the promotion of exports.

The new fashions were so full that some of the simpler frocks needed twenty and some even thirty yards of airy *tulle*. That spring, women revelled in femininity, adding an inch or two to their already 'absurdly high' heels, and wearing frills and sashes and ruffles and fichus, even hoops and bustles. In London, Lady

Above: Illustration, painted by George
Barbier in 1919, of the soldier's warm
welcome home at the end of the war. He
must have been surprised by the new
freedom in women's fashion. Not only
did he find a dress with a featherlight
short skirt, but it was backless too, both
ideas having been unheard of at the
beginning of the war. This painting
appeared in the 1920 *Guirlande des Mois*

Right: Paris took up the Tango again
with great enthusiasm and relief at the
end of the war. Backless dresses in fluid
fabrics made the dance even more *risqué*
and enjoyable. Illustration painted by
George Barbier in 1919, for the 1920
Guirlande des Mois

Cynthia Asquith noted in her diary in 1915, with some surprise,
that the war was giving her an unusually strong appetite for clothes
and that they had 'undergone enormous changes since the war and
have become practically early Victorian with really full skirts'.

In the spring of 1917, as if to brighten the lives of the war-weary,
Jules Meynial published the first of the five George Barbier
almanacs: *La Guirlande des Mois*. This delightful little silk-
bound book had beautifully printed *pochoir* illustrations designed
by Barbier and printed by Jean Saudé.

During the final battles of the last year of the war, fashion was
still a strong influence according to reports in the press; and the
reporters were not content with recording just that which a woman
wore, they insisted that it should extend to her figure, her com-
plexion, her state of mind and even her dog. 'Fancy,' declared one
editorial, 'carrying a short, full dog, when fashion insists on long
straight ones, it's like trying to combine an ornate *Louis Seize* style
dog with a *moyen-âge* gown, it simply couldn't be done.' It would
seem that if you loved fashion you must also love her dog, and a
fashionable lady of 1918 would have blushed to be seen with a
1913 model.

In 1919 the champagne-like bubbles of fashion were once again
rising to the surface in Paris. That spring, shorter skirts were the
sensation of the collections – for those whose figures were trim and
whose ankles were slender. The magazines revelled in femininity
and the leading editorials regained much of their former sparkle.
Baron de Meyer, the outstanding French photographer of the
period, captured the spirit of the time with some beautiful photographs, and two new *de luxe* edition magazines appeared with
pochoir fashion illustrations of pre-war quality, *La Guirlande* and
Les Feuillets d'Art. In London too the prospects of post-war
activities were luring the fashion journalists into excited prose.
Vogue considered the long-awaited pleasures of unlimited motoring
again 'when the bright procession shall speed once more to Epsom
and Henley and Newmarket, when the whole land, ringing with the
rhythm of the joy ride, shall put on its choicest greens, its loveliest
golds, to welcome the return of the car'.

The last collections of the decade were awaited with even more
than the usual interest, for they were also the first fashions since
the official signing of the peace treaty. These collections aroused
high expectations and by all reports the fashionable women of the
world were not disappointed by the new wizardry of *crêpe de Chine*,
taffeta and velvet. As for men's wear during this post-war period –
kings may have fallen and republics gone by the board, feminine
fashions could come and go, but neither age nor time could quell
the renewed mode for the 'shiny top hat and the neatly tailored
cutaway suit'.

The Golden Age of Style
1919-1925

The fashionable woman of 1920, having drunk a toast to the first New Year of a new decade, let her thoughts wander to the lengthening days, her social prospects, and inevitably to a new frock or two . . . As if to celebrate the birth of this new decade, a new magazine also appeared – *Art, Goût, Beauté*, which had a mixture of hand-coloured and half-tone tipped-in illustrations. In addition, the influential *Gazette du Bon Ton* resumed publication. In an earlier issue of the *Gazette*, a leading editorial had compared the contemporary flowering of the decorative arts with the spirit of the Italian Renaissance. Once again the *directeur*, Lucien Vogel, stated his belief in this modern renaissance which he thought was at work amongst the artists and designers of the western world.

Maurice Marinet and François-Émile Décorchemont were making glass objects. Jean Dunand developed and modernized the ancient oriental art of lacquering for screens and decorative panels; J-E Ruhlmann and Clément Mère made beautiful furniture in

Far left: An evening dress from the *haute couture* house of Jenny, painted by Brunelleschi for a 1920 edition of *Guirlande des Mois*. The illustration style is close to that developed before the war, although Brunelleschi added the appearance of a metallic shine to the legs, skirt and sash, and this was to become a frequent feature of fashion painting during the 1920s. The dress itself has the entirely new dropped waistline

69

la belle Torquatienne

Left: This design by Charles Martin, from the *Gazette du Bon Ton* of May 1920, exemplifies the new colours and sketchier style which were to creep into the fashion illustrations of the 1920s

Right: Suit and children's clothes designed by Jeanne Lanvin and painted for the *Gazette du Bon Ton* of October 1920, by Pierre Brissaud. Brissaud, who was one of the original artists on the *Gazette*, retained a more standard style of painting after the war

macassar ebony trimmed with shagreen and ivory; François-Louis Schmied designed, engraved and printed fabulous books; Camille Fauré made exquisitely coloured enamelled vases; Da Silva Bruhns was famous for stylish carpets; Baguès revived the medieval art of decorative wrought-iron work; Raoul Dufy designed and printed startlingly exotic fabrics; interior designers of the calibre of Albert Armand Rateau and Eileen Gray created wonderfully sophisticated settings for the display of Impressionist works, African art and Cubist paintings and sculpture. *Haute couture* designers had raised themselves up in the pre-war years from anonymity and were now ready to claim equal status with these other decorative artists, speaking of their work not only as a craft but in architectural and sculptural terms too. The *Gazette du Bon Ton* was sure that, in 1920, 'dress exemplified the spirit of its age' and that it was a 'true document of its time'.

This feeling for a new renaissance had been gradually developing since the Pre-Raphaelites had started their aesthetic movement in the mid-Victorian period. The unifying force of this movement

Above: Clever use of lighting and silhouette by André Marty in a 1919 illustration used in the 1921 album *Modes et Manières d'Aujourd'hui*. 'Le Ciné' shows Charlie Chaplin on the screen

Right: *The Essence of the Mode of the Day*, by Janine Aghian, from a series published in 1920. A model posed on such huge piles of cushions could have been found in pre-war fashion illustration, but here the human form has been simplified to an extreme degree, and the range of colours is harder and sharper than had been popular in the pre-war period

Above: In this illustration by André Marty which appeared in *Modes et Manières d' Aujourd' hui* in 1919, a disconcerted-looking Negro sculpture is watching the entrance of the fancy dress 'savages'. It was by this time very common for fashion illustrators to use humour to set off the fashions

was the desire to make things in an aesthetically honest way by using only the best natural materials available, applied with a complete mastery of the traditional methods of construction. And like *Art Nouveau, Art Déco* was based on this aesthetic philosophy of design integrity using the best natural materials and most highly skilled craftsmen regardless of the final cost.

This stylized form of refined luxury was pursued with a single-minded passion by all the artists and designers who created it, as well as by the fastidious clientele from all over the world who could afford the great expense involved. These ideals of exclusive luxury prevalent before the war did not, however, satisfy fully the visual aspirations of the *nouveaux riches*, nor did they reflect the general economic crisis existing in most European countries after the war. Paris, a year after the war, had retained its position as the Mecca for most of the modern artists and designers but had the atmosphere of a people in convalescence. Prices were rising alarmingly: sugar was scarce, butter was only sold on the black market, milk was forbidden in confectionery, wine was in short supply, the scarcity of meat provoked skirmishes at Les Halles and the shortage of electricity forced the government to stop the metro after eleven in the evening.

Above: A page from Charles Martin's successful experimental series for *Sports et Divertissements*, 1920, depicting a couple fishing near a bridge

In accordance with national traditions at such times of stress, grand pageants and gala spectaculars were mounted for all purposes, and of course, there was dancing . . . everybody danced. The dance halls were always full, the Tango and Fox-Trot reconquered the city, to be followed by the Black Bottom, the Shimmy and the Charleston, while the recently arrived American jazz bands played their loud, syncopated rhythms.

Day dresses might no longer be the formal affairs of before the war but evening gowns in 1921 were of unusual magnificence. They were luxurious works of decorative art, each being an exclusive and painstaking creation designed for a particular lady of society. Each was individually made, piece by piece, with linings and interlinings and boning and a thousand hooks and eyes. Fabrics already rich in themselves were not allowed to rest on their laurels, but were trimmed with fabulous gold lace and elaborate embroideries in beads and sequins and jewel-like stones.

Jewellery also flashed its costly message during this peak period of luxury, with the best in both fashion and jewellery being pursued with passionate determination by the fantastically wealthy beauties of the world – particularly South Americans and the few

Above: This page by Charles Martin is called 'Le Golf' and is also from *Sports et Divertissements* , of 1920. In the 1920s, illustration styles became more exacting, demanding much more of the reader than they ever had done previously. Charles Martin made a big contribution to these changes

Left: Pierre Brissand, in his very deft but rather conservative style, illustrated this scene for *L'Homme Élégant*, April 1921. The men's clothes are designed by George Harrison. The figure of the woman shows the less fussy and slimmer silhouette which developed in the early days of the 1920s

Right: A suit from the *haute couture* house of Beer illustrated by Benito for the May 1921 *Gazette du Bon Ton*. Such a suit became an increasingly important part of a woman's wardrobe, and its lines during the 1920s could be as smooth and lean as the lines of the greyhound itself. Benito's style of illustration was particularly well fitted to this more decisive fashion silhouette

Far right: Two women showing the straighter shapes which dominated the fashions of the 1920s painted by Marcelle Pichon for the *Gazette du Bon Ton*, July 1921. By this time fashion illustrators had plentiful outlets for their work and were firmly established. Their confidence becomes obvious in the way they freely distort and idealize the human shape

remaining *demi-mondaines* who still retained their pre-war lavishly extravagant sense of display. Jewellery was considered the supreme mark of achievement and every woman vied for individuality and distinctiveness in stones and settings to make the smartest possible statement of her way of life.

Magazines were fickle creatures during this period of stylistic change: they dared to like one thing on one day and another the following day, forgetting all about the day before yesterday and the novelties which had charmed them then. And among the fresh enchantments that journalists found to write about in 1922 was the redesigned jazz-age, jewel-coveting, cigarette-smoking, dance-loving, streamlined, modern woman. The new ideal of beauty was slenderness: to be plump was no longer fashionable. This new fashion in feminine shape with its straight-edged, rather harsh silhouette was in the same mould as the fashionable *Art Déco* style of design, as in the same way, the buxom, corseted curves of the Gibson Girls and the fashionable coquettes had echoed the taste for *Art Nouveau* during the *Belle Époque*.

GEORGE BARBIER 1

With this new shape of 'modern woman' came a new style of journalistic editorial. The words no longer flowed as in the traditions of the past; instead they 'were crisp and precise', 'witty and stylish', reflecting in prose the visual ideals of the designers of the period.

The more popular aspects of the press, however, did not fully succumb to this sophisticated editorial style, as the leader writers of London and New York still preferred the sensational reporting of scandals – 'the new audacious *décolletage*', 'the ever shortening skirt', all aroused their shocked indignation, as did 'the meagreness of the bathing costumes worn at the fashionable Brittany resorts' where 'those figure revealing costumes displayed by the daring created a sensation'. As well as creating a stir at these French resorts, particularly Dinard, the new-style bathing costumes also supplied many of the headlines, leading editorial and photographic interest of more than one major British and American popular newspaper.

But the little *cloche* hat turned out to be the biggest fashion story of the year. This very 1920s hat, with its rounded crown and its turned-down brim, was the hat that 'sat right in the eyes of the new fashions and attracted all the attention', reported the new *de luxe* magazine *Styl*. The next year this German *Art Déco* magazine

Left: George Barbier painted this for the August 1921, issue of the *Gazette du Bon Ton*, and characteristically chose to depict the harsher lines of the early 1920s against a lavish, curvilinear oriental background. This evening dress is designed by Worth, one of the oldest and most august *couture* houses in Paris at the time

Above left: A Venetian scene by George Barbier painted in 1921, and published in the 1922 *Falbalas et Fanfreluches*

Above right: A romantic moment on a dusky terrace, also painted by George Barbier in 1921 for *Falbalas et Fanfreluches*

Right: Charles Martin was very spirited in his contrived experiments with illustration. This page was done for an album promoting shoe designs by Pinet, and published in January 1922. Without ever caricaturing fashion, he managed to give it a zany, humorous life of its own

Far right: For the same 1922 Pinet album, Charles Martin painted this tea-time scene, again achieving liveliness and depth with minimal brush-work

had decided that 'just as surely as the women of yesterday were born to drive in a limousine, the woman of today was born to fly in an airoplane', and they wrote about the latest fashions of the air, such as a 'fur-lined mink-trimmed suit of thick suede', and a 'tight fitting *casque*' worn with 'soft boots strapped in puttee fashion' and a 'specially designed coat, side-fastened with front slit which buttons into trousers when preparing for flight but fastens flat when alighting'.

By 1923 one of the most unexpected signs of the changing times was the way in which day fashions were being steadily modified by this taste for sport, which became more and more pronounced as the decade progressed. Day dresses continued to be very smart, but at the same time they were becoming more functional, especially those for the younger, out-door girl. The unorthodox *haute couturière* Coco Chanel was the staunch supporter of this new style of youthful *chic*, promoting her designs by wearing them herself in the smart circles which she frequented. And with these smart, sporting clothes went the suntan, a fashionable accessory which

Left: Thayaht was best known for his illustrations of the designs of Madeleine Vionnet, which appeared in the *Gazette du Bon Ton* in the early 1920s. This one appeared in May 1922, and shows Vionnet's creation for the fortunate few who formed what would now be known as the 'jet set'. Flights between Croydon and Le Bourget made Paris fashions more readily accessible to Londoners, but as the aeroplanes and airports were more primitive than today, a warm, fur-lined travelling suit would have been especially welcome

Right: Another Madeleine Vionnet dress of remarkable originality matched by the intriguing illustration technique of Thayaht from the *Gazette du Bon Ton* of June 1922

Coco Chanel claims to have introduced, almost by accident, by letting her own South-of-France yachting tan be seen back in Paris. Her name, however, was to be almost synonymous with her short, slender woman's suit and although she produced new annual collections like other designers in Paris, she most of all, perhaps, remained unruffled by the clamour for more elaborate and novel fashions.

For evening wear, however, quite a different influence was at work, heightened by the discoveries made by Howard Carter and Lord Carnarvon in the tomb of Tutankhamun the previous year. Photographs and drawings of the wealth of finds in this ancient Egyptian tomb had an enormous impact on the decorative arts of the period, and among the fresh enchantments to be found that

Incantation

Au Polo.

autumn was a new style of fashionable decoration on clothes and accessories based on ancient Egypt. Together with the appearance of the scarab and hieroglyphs in the new designs of that period, the use of perfume and cosmetics was also given a tremendous boost by these discoveries urged on of course by numerous magazine editorials which stressed the exotic use of aromatics and facial decoration in the ancient world.

The following year a new influence was beginning to emerge in modern furniture from the relatively unknown *Bauhaus* school of design, which was to spread to fashion and fashion illustration and all the decorative arts. For it was their plain, logically-shaped tubular steel furniture, light fittings, textiles and graphics which were destined in the years ahead to change the current vogue for the luxurious *Art Déco* styles to the functional designs of *New Modernism*, and the more fluid streamlining of the 1930s.

In the world of entertainment the silver screen was increasing in popularity, the theatre staged marvellous productions, the *Ballets Russes* were as popular as ever – but it was the *Folies Bergère* which

Above left: Delicate and shimmering fabric has been used to make this summer dress illustrated by George Barbier for the 1924 edition of *Falbalas et Fanfreluches*

Far left: Inventive methods were often used to embellish the straight, tube-like evening dresses of the 1920s which were draped rather than tailored. The girl at the piano has her hair cropped in the style which in England was associated with 'arty' girls from the Slade, and elsewhere. This illustration by George Barbier was for the 1923 edition of *Falbalas et Fanfreluches*

Right: Sashes and wide picture hats were popular in the early 1920s, and dresses were cut or decorated to emphasize an angular quality which hid the natural curves of the body. This summer dress by Worth was painted by George Barbier for the *Gazette du Bon Ton* of August 1922

Far right: By 1924 the fashionable female silhouette was perfectly tubular; curves were out, and angular fabric patterns emphasized this. This painting was done by von Kabisch for a 1924 edition of the German periodical, *Styl*

created the major sensations in style and presentation in 1924. And above all with one spectacular production *Les Bijoux de Perles* designed by a young Russian, Romain de Tirtoff (better known as 'Erté'), which was created as a glittering showcase for beautiful young girls in seductive *déshabillé*. The following year it was the turn of the beautiful black American Josephine Baker to electrify Paris with her sensuous dancing in the *Revue Nègre*, whilst at the same time Erté set sail for Hollywood in the hope that he would be able to bring a new elegance to the film fashions of Metro-Goldwyn-Mayer.

The year of 1925 was also the year of the great Paris Exhibition of Decorative Arts, *Paris Exposition Internationale des Arts Décoratifs et Industriels Modernes*, which was the culminating point of *Art Déco* and from which the style took its name. The exhibition had originally been planned for 1915 to display the expensive

88

L'Eau

L'Automne

artifacts designed and made for a then small and fastidious clientele. By 1925, however, much of the luxurious splendour of the original *Art Déco* style had been replaced by more superficially designed items aimed at an ever increasing market. As *Art Déco* was gradually projected more and more towards this mass market it began to lose its identity, becoming permeated with the more superficial aspects of the style. This resulted for example in the Jazz Age patterns of the late twenties and early thirties, an *ad hoc* mixture, by undiscriminating manufacturers, of visual ideas copied from both *Art Déco* and New Modernism which is best described as *kitsch*.

The exhibition itself was held on the banks of the Seine from April to October 1925, with contributions from twenty-eight nations, including Russia, America, France, Great Britain, Holland and Turkey. The *Gazette du Bon Ton* published a special Golden Issue to mark the occasion, with particular reference to the *Pavillon de l'Élegance* which housed the work of the great *couturiers* of the period – the Callot Soeurs, Jenny, Lanvin and Worth – together with a spectacular display of jewellery by Cartier and luxurious

Far left: A new style of illustration, showing a hat designed by Marthe Collot, appeared in the January 1925 issue of the *Gazette du Bon Ton*; it was drawn by Zinoview

Above left: George Barbier continued to illustrate *Falbalas et Fanfreluches*, still incorporating features of the 'floating world' of Japanese art to enhance his style. This page, painted in 1925, appeared in the 1926 edition

Above right: An unashamedly sentimental picture by George Barbier for the 1926 edition of *Falbalas et Fanfreluches*. His signature, so prominently placed, is a measure of how fashion illustrators had lost their anonymity since the turn of the century

Above and far right: Lilies, chrysanthemums and roses painted by Paul Allier for *Les Fleurs*, an album published by Galerie Lutetia. Allier's faces convey a strong sense of mood in these charming little scenes, with a remarkably simple style of painting

furnishings by Rateau, Ruhlmann, Dunand and Baguès. This was to be one of the last issues of this beautiful magazine; it ceased publication in November of that year, having published sixty-nine issues since it first appeared in November 1912.

The entire exhibition was made up from original contemporary works, for under the conditions of entry the reproduction of old patterns or re-used designs was forbidden. On looking back at the official catalogues and magazine reports of the exhibition it is possible to see how some of the items on display highlighted the division of styles which was beginning to emerge between the luxury of *Art Déco* and the functionalism of New Modernism with the modernist movement beginning to make substantial progress. Thus although the best of the *Art Déco* pieces reached a peak of aesthetic excellence never before displayed in such abundance, at the same time this famous *Art Déco* exhibition marked the beginning of a new era of design that was anti-decoration, with a philosophy based on the belief that all things must be useful, and that beauty only exists in the functional.

LES CHRYSANTHÈMES

A New Fashion Image
1925-1932

The great Paris Exhibition of 1925 had finally uncorked fashion's ultra-smart '*moderne image*' and recharged the creative minds of the designers, as well as creating new desires in the hearts of their rich clientele. But no matter how inspired the *couturiers* were, the success of this new image hinged to a great extent on the *chic moderne* fabrics in eccentric geometric patterns and on the exquisitely-made accessories.

The word *chic*, which appeared over and over again in all sorts of publications throughout this period, summed up this new vogue. On looking at the magazines of fashion and the decorative arts of that period it is possible to see that originally the journalists and advertising writers were not entirely sure of what they meant when they used it, but they liked the look and the sound of this evocative four-letter word – '. . . A lovely skin is essentially *chic* . . .' '. . . A *chic*, youthful ensemble . . .' '. . . The new shorter bob is very *chic* . . .' '. . . Sequined dresses are *chic* for evening . . .' – and

Far left: A colourful impression of a crowd at the races which appeared in an album published for *La Grande Maison de Blanc*, painted by Rojan. It not only shows the shape of fashion, but the background shows just how much of modern art styles fashion illustration had absorbed by the late 1920s

Art - Goût - Beauté

Left: Dresses designed by Drecoll and
Paquin painted by Collette for the June
1926 issue of *Art, Goût, Beauté.* These
low-waisted, short dresses worn with
close-fitting cloche hats were constantly
described by the fashion journalists of
the day as very 'chic'

Right: From *Art, Goût, Beauté* of June
1926, these luxurious designs by Jean
Patou were illustrated by Leon Benigni.
Chic hairstyles were short and shining,
dresses exploited subtle colour contrasts.
These designs indicate the widening
difference between evening and day
wear. By this time women were sporting
racey and very short dresses in the
daytime

applied it indiscriminately to everything from cami-knickers to
motor cars.

The far-from-dumb-blonde American heroine of Anita Loos'
exceptionally funny and popular, 1926 novel *Gentlemen Prefer
Blondes*, quickly grasped the importance of this new word. 'I mean
French is really very easy for instance the French use the word
"sheik" for everything while we only seem to use it for gentlemen

Right: A lively painting by Paul Allier, for *Estampes pour votre chambre* published by Galerie Lutetia. Allier favoured strong, bright colours and definite outlines in his illustrations

Far right: An autumn scene by Paul Allier, also for *Estampes pour votre chambre*

when they seem to resemble Rudolf Valentino.'

In the spring of 1926, several of the major international magazines also featured the architecture of Le Corbusier which they thought would revolutionize the way in which we lived. Already well known for his sensational pavilion, 'L'Esprit Nouveau', at the 1925 decorative arts exhibition, Le Corbusier had just completed a house built entirely of white concrete, suggestive of a steamship in shape and simple, unfussy and very streamlined inside. This bold design suggested many exciting possibilities for the architecture which was to follow and it also raised many questions about the aesthetic standards and beauty of buildings, whether domestic, commercial or municipal. Le Corbusier's theories did not find immediate or widespread support but they eventually produced a general modification of architectural styles which resulted in some of the most satisfying and successful buildings of the 1930s.

Surrealism was another subject about which controversy raged throughout the 1920s and '30s and which is debated still. However, unlike other advances in painting such as Cubism, certain aspects of Surrealism lent themselves easily to the applied arts and to

fashion. Visual puns and shocks, which were central to the impact of Surrealism, could easily be transposed from one medium to another and when Salvador Dali collaborated with the *haute couturière* Schiaparelli in 1938, he designed a fabric patterned with purple tears to create the sensation that parts of the dress were hanging down in shreds. In complete contrast to the controversies over Surrealism or the work of Le Corbusier, some magazine editorials continued to record ephemeral whims of fashion. In Autumn 1926, they noted that artificial flowers were once again in fashion: enormous roses, gardenias and marguerites for *robes tailleurs* and exotic gold and silver carnations or royal blue lilies for afternoon dresses.

On looking through the magazines of the period – *Femina*, *Harper's Bazar*, *La Femme Chic* or *Vogue*, or a copy of *Art, Goût, Beauté*, the only remaining fashion magazine with hand-coloured illustrations – one is above all struck by the simplicity of line of those longer-than-life young ladies, with their short, tubular dresses, cigarettes in long black holders, *cloche* hats, bobbed hair

Below: Highly imaginative and idealized dresses depicted in a summer scene by Paul Allier for an album published by Galerie Lutetia and called *Les Quatre Saisons*

and bands of diamond bracelets, who symbolized the visual aspirations of the New Modernist styles.

The aesthetics of this new, smart image were quite different from those of only twenty-five years earlier. Had one of the fashionable ladies from the turn of the century gone for an afternoon walk along the rue de la Paix, Bond Street or Fifth Avenue in 1927, her freshly-washed, unpowdered face would have been the only one thus exposed to the public eye. In her beruffled dress and fineries, she would wonder what new race had come to inhabit the earth, for all the women would have looked emaciated by comparison with her full curves. For above all, the meagreness of the new mode would have amazed her, a meagreness accentuated by the fashionably bustless, reed-like figure and the short skirts.

In the autumn of 1927, for the first time in the recorded history of the western world, women's knees became an accepted and respectable sight in fashionable society. But it was not long before disparaging comments were being written about those knees and the plain garters most women wore to keep their stockings from

Below: Paul Allier's version of springtime, painted for *Les Quatre Saisons* published in an album by Galerie Lutetia

Right: A painting by Tito entitled '*Qui trop embrasse*' from a de-luxe album called *Quatre Proverbes*. The gracefully erotic image has been framed within the open windows

wrinkling. 'Novelty garters' were the answer, and they soon appeared in all shapes, sizes and colours, to be worn either above the knee or below, and always to draw attention to the wearer's legs. Of the many other changes that were taking place, none was more dramatic than that connected with lingerie. The woman from the *Belle Époque* would have had a cupboard full of voluminous snowy white linen, while the smart young things had but a few sets of colourful cami-knickers and princess slips, and in place of the innumerable tucks, decorative stitchery, insertions and flounces that had adorned the underwear of the 1900s, the undergarments of the late 1920s were absolutely simple sets, made in spun silk, tussore, *crêpe-de-Chine*, georgette or artificial silk.

The young men about London – those who frequented clubs like White's or Bucks, took their cocktails at Masters and dined at the Embassy – showed a very high standard of dress throughout this period, and between 1926 and 1932 magazines of quality praised the 'English pre-eminence in men's fashion', convinced that it was quite unshakable – to the despair and confusion of those tailors and *chemisiers* in Paris who made 'tight, form-moulding clothes', and 'brightly-hued accessories'. With the exception of evening dress, formal afternoon clothes were considered the most important in a man's wardrobe: a top hat, cutaway coat, striped trousers and of course spats.

As well as clothes, the motor car was of major importance to the young 'man about town' in the twenties, not to mention the 'young flapper'. Unfortunately, by 1928 the expense of keeping up the fashionable larger cars – the English Rolls-Royce, the Italian Isotta-Fraschini Cabriolet, the American Packard, the German eight-cylinder Horch or the luxurious Hispano-Suiza – had passed the point of possibility for all but the very rich and the Midases of the movies. However, invention came to the rescue of the gay young things with the 'two-dog-power cars' produced by Bugatti, Renault, Citroen and the new AC sports model which even had a dicky large enough for the fashionable borzoi.

Beauty was another major preoccupation, not only for the aspiring young woman but for men too. The mixed beauty salon had been introduced via American magazines to cater for this aspect of the modern way of life. Advertisements carried the message: 'Ladies be beautiful. Intelligence is deceitful. Amiability is useless

Left: A painting called '*Le Divan*', by
Edouard Halouze, in an album of
illustrations solely by him, showing the
most sleek and daring woman of fashion

Right: 'Smoking' appeared in an album
aptly named *Femmes Modernes*.
Chompré, the artist, has depicted a truly
modern and independent woman, with
cropped hair and eye make-up. Not only
does such a modern woman smoke, but
she is shown here lounging in a posture
no woman of the *Belle Époque* could have
believed

and Virtue is vain. If you want to please the strong, strenuous,
silent male, looks are your only bait – Be lovely or lose him.' And
for men: 'The old, vaunted masculine supremacy is gone for ever.
You are beaten, outwitted, outvoted, outplayed and outstripped.
You have lost the privilege of being ugly. All you have left is your
charm. So make the most of it – Get pretty or beat it.' All that was
needed, it would seem, was the price of ten sittings at a Mixed
Beauty Salon, to guarantee the desirable look of a 'Lounge Lizard'
or a 'Gimmy Girl'.

American-style beauty, as depicted in the Hollywood films of
the late twenties, had become really big business. 'Automobiles,
Movies and Bootlegging are the three biggest American industries,'
said one editorial of 1928, 'but after these comes the beauty
business.' If one looks through the advertisement pages of any

popular American magazine of that period you will find that at least one page in every three was devoted to beauty. Soaps, skin-foods, lotions, hair-preservers and hair-removers, powder, paints, pastes, pills that dissolved fat from the inside, bath salts that dissolved it from without and foods that were guaranteed not to make you fat at all, machines that gave massages and exercised the muscles and other more complicated machines that gave electric shocks to tone up the muscles without exercise.

Elizabeth Arden and Helena Rubenstein must take a lot of the credit not only for expanding the cosmetics industry but for pioneering safe products which more often than not actually did what they said they would do. From Arden and Rubenstein's ambitious competition with each other grew the idea of a beauty salon and the beauty experts and specialists, the masseurs and the

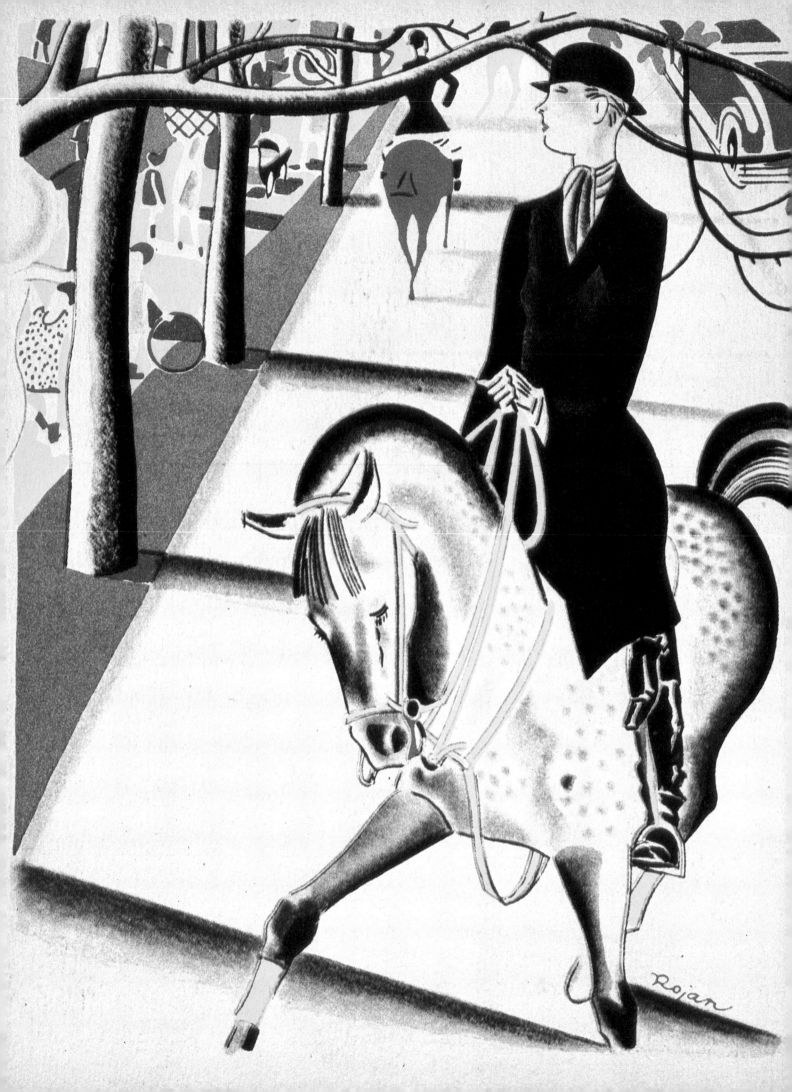

masseuses . . . the list is legion and the legions prospered.

In the autumn of 1929 the Patou Collection dropped the hemline and reintroduced waists, creating a sensation after the almost standard above-the-knee skirts and waist-at-the-hips silhouette of the past few years. Chanel's designs hit the floor of her salon but a few seconds later, and one of the memorable revolutions of the fashion world had been accomplished when it was reported that 'all the women were squirming about in their chairs tugging at the hems of their skirts'. Hollywood found itself left with a stock of pictures in which there was a great deal of unintentional comedy, as the famous stars parading with visible knees suddenly became *démodé*. The financial losses this created in the film industry were, however, to some extent offset by the fortunes about to be made from the newly introduced 'talkies'.

Upon the very tick of the spring equinox of 1930 the fashionable magazines in London, Paris and New York blossomed with the most exciting collection of feminine fashion seen for many years. They proclaimed that the 'hard, crisp, shiny, *chic* era' of the nineteen-twenties woman, with her Eton crop and short skirt, was dead. How marvellous it would be, they thought, to be naked with a cheque-book 'to be able to start from scratch at the beginning of this new decade, with the latest feminine fashions' . . . 'to put on nothing but the new, new, new'.

During the last few months of 1929 and the first few months of 1930 a silent and bloodless revolution had taken place among the *couturiers*, designers, stylists and their smart clientele, a revolution directed against the severe angularities of the modernist style of design. In furnishings, curves made a return, replacing the straight lines of the recently fashionable glass and metal pieces. In dress, soft draperies, flowing gracefully from beautifully tied bows, were taking the place of the severe straightness of the 'bright young boy' styles. Hair was beginning to be softly waved and loosely curled; complexions were young and pretty, without eccentricities. The fashionable society of Europe and America had recovered from the shock of the Wall Street crash of the previous October, and once again the gaiety of spring was in the air.

Left: Illustration of riders in the Paris woods by Rojan for an album published for *La Grande Maison de Blanc*. A blue car passes across the top corner of the scene

The fashionable figure was still slender, but now the natural shape could be displayed with the dress flowing softly over the body curves, clinging to the figure from the natural waist to just below the hips. Above this the dresses were slightly bloused whilst they widened below the hips and flowed softly to between mid-calf and ankle-length, often with inset flared panels of very intricate cut.

With such a dramatic change in feminine fashion, from the crisp *chic* look of the late nineteen-twenties to the more glamorous outlook of the early thirties, the well-dressed woman could no longer just happen, as if she had been turned out of a designer's mould. She pored over designs, fingered fabrics, tried on hats and considered the new accessories critically. Fashion was no longer classified by the press as a purely feminine preoccupation; it was

varie. Sur les unes la taille est indiquée par des pinces, sur les autres par des ceintures de cuir ou de même tissu.

Encolures et Paletots

Les cols se nouent de côté en cravate et marient souvent deux teintes d'une même fourrure, laquelle est toujours à poil ras, hermine, astrakan, agneau rasé, lapin et rat. Très chic en son aspect sportif le paletot en peau de vache très assouplie : en nuance tourterelle, sur jupe et corsage de même ton, il a énormément d'allure et convient surtout aux gentilles « chauffeuses » qui conduisent elles-mêmes leur six-

ETINCELLE. — *Ensemble de velours imprimé.*
Création Worth

PILE OU FACE. — *Ensemble d'après-midi en crêpe satin "Bellita" A.G.B. et lainage.*
Création Lucile Paray

Left: Paray and Worth designs, illustrated by Dory for the fine fashion periodical *Art, Goût, Beauté*, in October 1929. This is one of the last moments for short skirts; as share prices on Wall Street fell, so did the hemline. But the soft diagonal lines of these dresses continued into the 1930s

Right: *Art, Goût, Beauté* continued its high standards of fashion illustration into the new decade. This page shows designs by Jenny, Patou and Martial et Armand, painted by Bacly for the issue of December 1931. With the new longer skirts the waist returned to its natural position, but the emphasis remained on the hips

EN FAVEUR. — Vêtement de ratine avec fourrure de karakul. Le col donne un mouvement d'écharpe croisée en gilet. Découpes incrustées. Le bas du devant, côté fermeture, est coupé en biseau.

Création MARTIAL & ARMAND.

COTE D'AZUR. — Manteau pour le sport en tweed moucheté avec bandes de cuir. Col Danton souple. Grandes poches retenues dans un encadrement incrusté.

Création JENNY.

TOUT VA BIEN. — Manteau de tout aller élégant en lainage fantaisie garni de loutre. Les manches sont étroites du haut et de forme gigot du coude aux poignets avec travail de nervures.

Création MARTIAL & ARMAND.

FIORETTI. — Manteau d'après midi en tissu vigogne noir paré d'astrakan du même ton. La fourrure est posée en découpes au bord du manteau. Elle recouvre la moitié des manches et le col droit.

Création JEAN PATOU.

Right: Two designs by Worth, shown
here on four mannequins in the
September 1932 issue of *Art, Goût,
Beauté*, painted by Baldrich. The cloche
hat still found favour, but was worn at
an increasingly tilted angle, until it no
longer resembled its 1920s predecessor

Far right: Charles Martin evoked the
earlier, more fanciful illustration styles
of the 1920s in this scene from a bullring
which formed part of a Christmas
supplement to *Art, Goût, Beauté* in 1931

being considered as one of the art forms of its time.

In the dress collections the following spring, the distinguishing
marks of the newest designs were vivid colours used in strong contrasts. Success with this new arrangement was not easy, for a
wrong balance of opposing tones could easily create a look of
vulgarity which at that time was the antithesis of the new, glamorous fashions. The liking for strong colour contrasts was also seen
in the new summer hats, the new shapes accentuating the latest
colour arrangements. The most striking hat shapes had wide brims,
usually with an irregular droop cleverly arranged to display only
one side of the wearer's face. The Frenchwoman, with her large
eyes, rounded face and small bones, was able to 'wear these hats
triumphantly'. But they were not so easy to wear for the average
English or American woman, who generally thought of hats as a
pretty frame for the face.

In the autumn, it was reported, women were going to look even
taller. At one house after another, dresses were being shown which
gave the look of a long, straight silhouette with lots of fullness at the
hem. This new shape was achieved by interesting sectional cutting

108

Right: Versions of two designs by
Martial et Armand illustrated by
Baldrich for *Art, Goût, Beauté*,
September 1932

with bias panels, so that the frocks flowed over the body and
rippled into sufficient fullness at the hem, with never a pleat or a
gather to show how it was done. Madeleine Vionnet was the great
expert on this new way of cutting. No other dressmaker had ever
had her understanding of the human form, whilst her mastery of
fabric was uncanny. Her bias-cut frocks and gowns had a simplicity
of line and a grace of movement which was Grecian in spirit, yet
they were amazingly intricately cut, with crossway sections which,
partly through the quality of stretching which this method of
cutting gave, moulded the figure of the wearer and then draped
about her limbs in a peculiarly elegant way before flowing almost
like liquid to the floor.

Many Englishwomen travelled to Paris by air to see the Vionnet
and other collections or to buy the latest decorative novelty. The
newly introduced day-trip to Paris by Imperial Airways 'Argosies'
was surprisingly quick and easy. Passengers were at Croydon in
time for breakfast, at Le Bourget for coffee and in the heart of Paris
for an early luncheon. From then until late tea there was time to
do some shopping, see a dress show and meet one's friends before

Left: Page by Baldrich for *Art, Goût, Beauté*, September 1932, showing the sharply angled hats and beautifully tailored clothes popular throughout the 1930s. The red dress clearly indicates the exacting standards required in tailored clothes, an entirely different technique from the more loosely draped designs of the 1920s

a rapid journey back from Paris to Croydon in just over two hours. There was no customs rush, just an easy stroll through the terminal to one's waiting car, and then home in time for dinner.

By 1932 the CIAM or *Congrès Internationaux d'Architecture Moderne*, formed four years earlier by Le Corbusier and his contemporaries, was making remarkable progress, as was the *Bauhaus* School which by then had moved to Dessau. Their combined influence on industrial aesthetics was growing stronger daily as their ideas developed into the reality of architecture and manufactured designs. America was in the forefront of this new development, and the American press, together with the European, published many new ideas in books and magazines, explaining the new aesthetic theories and how these could be applied to modern life. It was thought that modern industry was the driving force of the new age and that the object of the industrial designer was to use all the resources of the new age to make life more convenient, comfortable and congenial . . . Unfortunately most of the items manufactured during this period were decorated 'slang' versions of the modern designs the authors and editors were writing about, and directly opposed to the spirit of the truly modern industrial designs of the time. These items should therefore be classified alongside Victorian *bric-à-brac* in that they have most of the faults of that great mid-nineteenth-century period of visual atrocities about which the Pre-Raphaelites felt so strongly.

In the world of fashion, 1932 was relatively uneventful. The spring clothes were feminine, practical and marvellously easy to wear. Skirt lengths stayed about where they were, varying just a little according to the type and proportion of the dress. The summer frocks had a romantic look and in the autumn little jacketed suits were popular. For evening the accent was on beautifully cut dresses with a softly flowing silhouette which were worn with fabulous jewellery.

Towards the end of the year the last issue of the stylish *Art, Goût, Beauté*, with its tipped-in hand-coloured fashion illustrations, was published. Thus, after a period of twenty-five years, the great age of 'illustrated style' had now come to an end. A quarter of a century had elapsed since the first design folder illustrated by Paul Iribe for Paul Poiret in *Les Robes de Paul Poiret* in 1908 which together with *Les Choses de Paul Poiret*, *Modes et Manières d'Aujourd'hui*, *Journal des Dames et des Modes*, *Gazette du Bon Ton*, *La Guirlande des Mois*, *Falbalas et Fanfreluches*, *Art, Goût, Beauté*, and many other magazines, folders and periodicals, had captured the visual excellence of the period. Fortunately the style of these illustrations was not completely lost, as many of the artists continued working for quality magazines such as the American *Harper's Bazar* or the newly introduced English *Harper's Bazaar*, the English, American and French editions of *Vogue* and the French *Femina* and *La Femme Chic*, but the quality of the illustrations which had formerly been produced by the elaborate hand-printed *pochoir* process has never again been equalled. These illustrations remain as a fitting tribute to their creators, and to the artists, designers and craftsmen with whom they worked, during those twenty-five creative years.

Septembre 1932

Prix du Numéro : France **10** Fcs

Art . Goût G . Beauté

LES RÉGATES A SOCOA

FEUILLETS
DE
L'ÉLÉGANCE FÉMININE
PARIS

13e Année - No 145

The End of an Epoch
1932-1939

Throughout the twenties and early thirties the designers of the more fashionable aspects of the decorative and applied arts, together with the great dressmakers, would have denied that films and film-star fashions had much influence on major design developments of that period. They might have conceded that individual stars such as Clara Bow, Mary Pickford and Gloria Swanson had introduced a new type of 'glamorous' look into every film-goer's life, and that they had helped to promote new design ideas, but they did not initiate completely new fashions as such. By 1933, the influence of the glamorous Hollywood stars, Marlene Dietrich, Greta Garbo, Norma Shearer, Joan Crawford, Ruby Keeler and Claudette Colbert, together with Adrian, the great Hollywood designer, was undeniable. Gone were the days when the latest fashion ideas could be gleaned only by attending an exclusive dress parade; now it was possible for everybody to have access to the most up-to-date fashions by going to the pictures.

Far left: The Hollywood image was absorbed by Paris designers and remoulded in their own inimitable style. These two evening dresses by *couturier* Robert Pignet were photographed for the French fashion magazine *L'Officiel* during the autumn collections of 1938

Right: Dress designed by the London *couturier* Victor Stiebel shown in a photograph which also featured the latest taste in furniture. The close links which often exist between fashion and interior decoration are shown here, at the beginning of the new decade, with particular clarity

In order to sustain this newly acquired fashionable image, the big Hollywood studios paid enormous annual dress bills which would have given a permanent headache to the richest and most indulgent of husbands in the *Belle Époque*. Even in the mid-thirties, the days of Jean Harlow and the other popular exponents of the 'great underdressed' ideals of feminine fashion, it cost some studios over a million pounds each year to clothe the beauties of filmland in the luxury to which the fans were accustomed.

In the traditional world of *haute couture* this new film influence tended to confuse some journalists. 'There was a time when fashion writers could say just what was what . . . which meant that was *it* . . . but in these days the matter isn't quite so simple. After a long course of viewing the latest Dress Collections I feel inclined to say that anything is fashionable so long as it is glamorous.'

Left: An early 1930s photograph by
Baron De Meyer for *Harper's Bazaar*,
of a satin dress by Cheruit. It captures
the fluid look of the period

The renewed glitter in the Champs Elysées in the autumn of
1933 highlighted the welcome return of a reasonable amount of
financial stability which had been badly shaken by the Wall Street
crash of 1929. As the cars swept up and down that famous
highway, women were preparing for a winter of glamour and
elegance of a kind that many had feared was gone forever. The new
silhouette followed the shape of the figure very closely, moulding
the bust and hips, whilst below the knees skirts were much wider
and more often than not they were decoratively trimmed.

The lingerie worn with these figure-hugging dresses had to be
as beautifully cut as the dresses themselves, or it would have spoilt
the outlines of the smooth clinging silhouette. As the lines of the
dresses changed, so did those of the garments worn under them.
The tendency was for simplicity of line, with knickers and slips cut

on the cross so that they stretched to fit like a glove and yet did not drag. As skirts became more figure-hugging the knickers became shorter, yet remained open-legged 'leaving only a wisp of fabric protecting female modesty'. Sometimes lace trimmed the edges; others had beautiful inset motifs and embroidered net panels with hand-worked open stitches.

'Forwards! Backwards! Downwards!' were the major fashion headlines for '34. Unmistakably a new element was sweeping into fashion. The new profile was streamlined: some waists were pinched in with a belt, shoulders were wide but not square or mannish; even more noticeable was the return of the narrow skirt, with many garments featuring an open slit at the hem for ease and comfort. By the mid-season, more changes were to come: 'Snip, Slit, Slash, Scissors have been cutting recklessly through the skirts of the summer collections.' Incisions had been made in front, at the back and on both sides. They were cut from a few inches to twelve or more, laying open a substantial expanse of ankle and shin-bone – 'another inch and knees would once again have been out in public'. On *décolletages*, also, scissors had been at work. 'Down in the front' seems to have been the general cry. Lelong cut some of his dresses almost to the waist. Augustrabernard's *décolletages* disclosed the swell of the breasts. Away with shoulder-straps said Mainbocher, whilst Schiaparelli lowered her necklines precariously close to the limit of modesty.

Paris *haute couture*, maybe reflecting the rumours of a 'Royal Romance' between Princess Marina of Greece and the Duke of Kent, gave the world a 'Romantic Autumn Collection'. By day it was nicely restrained, but at night picturesque romanticism broke wildly loose. At Vionnet's the new feeling reached its highest pitch in a mythical cavalcade to which all the heroines of history had come with their dresses beautifully metamorphosed into those of 1934. But side by side with romantic crinolines, Molyneux's streamlined silhouette was to be seen. Directoire suits rubbed shoulders with simple, box-like modernities. Cossack hats towered opposite shallow pill-boxes, peasant sleeves alongside skin-tight ones, extra-long trains near knee-exposing slits, and bustle-ish dresses next to moulded bodies, with no one silhouette overpowering the rest.

By 1935 the big beauty break-through came with the development and general acceptance of make-up, mainly due to the Hollywood publicity machine which marketed glamour, sex appeal, make-up and beauty as an essential part of modern fashion. Everybody was asked to notice the rare beauty of the Hollywood Stars, all of whom used skilfully applied make-up to help 'increase their magnetism as they blazed into brilliant stardom'.

As a result of the great financial disaster of 1929 and the subsequent industrial slump, commercial rather than private patronage was responsible for the major *Art Déco* commissions in the thirties. In America, for example, in addition to filmland's own 'Hollywood *Déco*' style, the designs for Radio City in New York were commissioned from J-E Ruhlmann. In England a combination

Right: The best of English tailored fashions photographed in 1934. An immediate international appeal was lent to this photograph by the use of the Imperial Airways 'Argosy'

Below: Dramatic hat photographed against an equally dramatic background for *Harper's Bazaar* in 1934, showing the improvement in fashion photography which produced some exceptionally powerful images during the 1930s

of Hollywood inspired *Déco* with fairyland fantasy was the style used for the new Odeon Cinemas, which were specifically designed to heighten the audiences' sense of well-being while they lost themselves in the celluloid world of imported glamour.

Perhaps the most elaborate official commission was that for the extravagant *décor* for the French luxury liner the *Normandie*, which was designed to give every passenger that feeling of luxurious elegance normally reserved to a film star or a millionaire's mistress. The cabins were luxurious, the halls and *salons* beautifully proportioned and decorated. The main *salon* with its black and gold tapestries, its paintings on glass by Jean Dupas, its beautiful Aubusson carpets; the bar with its immense gold lacquer decorations by Jean Dunand, the fabrics by Rodier and curtains by Colcombet; the golden staircase leading to the grill . . . all were a magnificent tribute to the great French decorative artists of the period, as were the magnificently dressed and bejewelled celebrities who sailed on the maiden voyage in June 1935.

The *Normandie* quickly became the most fashionable way to travel and it was much used that autumn by the American buyers who flocked to London and Paris to see what the great dressmakers had to offer. In Paris they found that the bosom was once again the main focal point of fashion and the *couturiers* had used all kinds of tricks to emphasize this most feminine of features. In London the dress shows had the unexpected excitement of a grand theatrical production. There were personal invitations and reserved seats, and photographers were everywhere snapping well-known actresses

Above: Marlene Dietrich posing between 'takes' in 1936. While the photograph was part of a French magazine feature about filmstars' legs, like many other photographs of the decade it helped to advertise the fashions born of the American film industry and encourage their popularity

Left: Jean Harlow, photographed in 1935. Her dress epitomizes the clinging, fluid style of glamorous film star fashions. Hollywood's influence in promoting this softer, more feminine image was in competition with other harsher, tailored styles during the mid-1930s, styles which *Vogue* dubbed 'hard-hearted' chic

Right: Suit by Henry Creed, with a hat by Rose Valois. This is typical of the photographs of the mid-1930s which promoted expensive English clothes for the international market by linking them with expensive English life-styles, and by using models whose very faces echoed the cool confidence of the high-quality tailoring

and society beauties. 'London Fashions' were now being sought out by the smartest American women. They were buying their suits there because they were 'London tailored' and their dresses and blouses because they were 'so English', with a unique, 'well-bred carelessness' appropriate to their new international way of life.

The following spring, if we are to believe one news reporter, a surprise was in store for the unwary bachelor. It would seem that if he was taking a young lady out to lunch she would quite possibly arrive having made herself more interesting 'with white eyelids and green eyelashes'. If, however, he was taking her for afternoon tea, things might have been worse, as she was likely to turn up with

Right: Fashion at the Tower of London during the first days of the Second World War, before the introduction of clothes rationing for the British. This typical English tailored suit, although an original design from the autumn *couture* collections of 1939, reflects the shape of the fashions which, of necessity, were to prevail almost throughout the war years

'blue finger-nails and blue toe-nails', a newly shortened skirt which 'displayed her rouged knees' and cutaway shoes designed to 'display her heels, which were also blushing with make-up'. If he had decided to ask her out to dinner, she would certainly turn up wearing an impossible hat, 'with birds, bunches of flowers and assorted fruit, reminiscent of an exotic greenhouse'. This writer decided that 'the feminine outlook was hopeless', with the exception of Schiaparelli's edible buttons, which constituted 'real progress' – especially if the occasion was to be a picnic.

During the summer of 1936, travel between the continents of the world became both quicker and easier. The great airlines were extending their services with the 32-passenger *Fokker XXXVI* and the *New Empire* flying-boat; the *Queen Mary* had made her maiden voyage to New York and back and the newest airship the *Hindenburg* was coming into regular service. Lakehurst, New Jersey to Frankfurt in forty-eight hours; Frankfurt to Rio in eighty; San Francisco to Manila in fifty-eight . . . only a few years earlier these schedules would only have been acceptable in a book by H. G. Wells.

Between 1936 and 1939 civilization witnessed a succession of world-shattering events . . . As the storm clouds of war were gathering over Europe, as if in one last gesture of defiance, 'all the glory that was Paris and all the grandeur that was London' were mustered for the last fashion collections of the decade.

In the autumn of 1939, as the opposing armies were gathering themselves for the bitter conflict to come, the designers launched their latest fashions. The new designs developed the very feminine silhouette which had been introduced in the spring. This was used by most journalists as a welcome relief from the depressing news which had surrounded the start of the Second World War. 'Do you like the thought of yourself with a tiny waist and high round breasts?' . . . 'Do you want to be more alluring than you have been for years?' . . . Then, they said, 'You will love the new dresses; Mainbocher's sensational moulded dresses; Balenciaga's hour-glass silhouette; Schiaparelli's cigarette slimness; Chanel's seductively curved hips; Lanvin's tempting *décolletages*; Molyneux's streamlined all-black evening gowns and Alix's revolutionary figure-revealing designs.' The secret of all this sex-appeal and pure seductiveness was in the old-fashioned boned and laced corset which had 'been made by modern magic', with the aid of the new technology.

But because of the war, clothes rationing, the occupation of France, austerity regulations and general shortages, this new, very feminine fashion had to be put aside for a number of years until it was revived in 1946, when 'Fashion Revels in Femininity' once again hit the headlines. This six-year delay changed some aspects of the silhouette launched in 1939, but in essence the post-war 'New Look' – as it was later to be called when shown by Christian Dior in the spring of 1947 – caught the spirit of this fashion and captured the interest of a public tired of austerity. That winter of 1939 saw much that changed the fashionable attitudes in all of the decorative arts from those of the early thirties; but those who are interested in the evolution of fashion and in the deeper sociological implications of changing design styles cannot help but wonder what changes might have occurred had war not broken out on 3rd September 1939.

Right: Evening dress and coat by Coco Chanel, from her autumn collection of 1938, and photographed with studied care in her Paris salon. Photographs such as this, composed and lit to emphasize the mood of the clothes, could be an important advertisement for the designers when they were featured in international fashion magazines

Collections

Among the libraries in which the limited-edition publications mentioned in this volume may be found are the following:

British Museum, London: *Femina, Gazette du Bon Ton, Journal des Dames et des Modes*
Bodleian Library, University of Oxford: *Gazette du Bon Ton*
Brooklyn Museum Library, New York: *La Femme Chic*
Free Library of Philadelphia: *Gazette du Bon Ton*
Harvard University Library, Cambridge, Massachusetts: *Modes et Manières d'Aujourd'hui*
Metropolitan Museum of Art Library, New York: *La Femme Chic, Gazette du Bon Ton, Journal des Dames et des Modes*
New York Public Library: *Art, Goût, Beauté, Femina, La Femme Chic, Gazette du Bon Ton, Journal des Dames et des Modes, Modes et Manières d'Aujourd'hui, Vogue*

United States Library of Congress, Washington: *Femina, Gazette du Bon Ton, Journal des Dames et des Modes*
University Library, University of Cambridge: *Gazette du Bon Ton*
Victoria & Albert Museum, London: *Art, Goût, Beauté, Falbalas et Fanfreluches, Femina, La Femme Chic, Gazette du Bon Ton, Journal des Dames et des Modes, Les Modes, Vogue*
Westminster Central Reference Library, London: *Journal des Dames et des Modes*

Art, Goût, Beauté was known between 1933 and 1936 as *Voici La Mode, Art, Goût, Beauté*. *Journal des Dames et des Modes* should not be confused with a periodical of the same name which appeared from 1797 to 1837. *Vogue* was first published in the U.S.A. in 1892, in London in 1916 and in France in 1921.

Bibliography

Battersby, M., *The Decorative Thirties* (Studio Vista, London 1971; Walker & Co., New York 1971; Macmillan, New York 1975)
Battersby, M., *The Decorative Twenties* (Studio Vista, London 1969; Walker & Co., New York 1969)
Beaton, C., *The Glass of Fashion* (Weidenfeld & Nicolson, London 1954)
Bliss, D. P., *The Stencil Process in France and England* (The Penrose Annual, London 1930)
Cocteau, J. & Alexandre, A., *Decorative Art of Léon Bakst* (London 1913, also Dover Publications, New York 1973)
Ewing, E., *History of Twentieth-Century Fashion* (Batsford, London 1974; Charles Scribner's Sons, New York 1975)
Garland, M., *The Indecisive Decade – the World of Fashion and Entertainment in the Thirties* (Macdonald, London 1968)
Haedrich, M., *Coco Chanel – (Her Life, Her Secrets)* (translated by C. L. Markham for Robert Hale & Co., London 1972)
Laver, J., *Women's Dress in the Jazz Age* (Hamish Hamilton, London 1964)
Lynam, R. (Ed.), *Paris Fashion: The Great Designers and their Creations* (Michael Joseph, London 1972, published as *Couture* by Doubleday, New York 1972)
Percival, J., *The World of Diaghilev* (Studio Vista, London 1971; Dutton, New York 1971)
Poiret, P., *My First Fifty Years* (London 1931)
Saudé, J., *Traité d'Enluminure d'Art au Pochoir* (Paris 1925)
Schiaparelli, E., *Shocking Life* (Dent, London 1954)
Torrens, D., *Fashion Illustrated: a review of Womens' dress 1920–1950* (Studio Vista, London 1974; Hawthorn Books Inc., New York 1975)
Traphagen, E., *Costume Design and Illustration* (first edition London and New York 1918, second edition 1932)
Veronesi, G., *Into the Twenties: style and design 1909–1929* (Thames & Hudson, London 1968; published as *Style and design 1909–1929* by Braziller, New York 1968)

Waugh, N., *Cut of Women's Clothes: 1600–1930* (Faber & Faber, London 1968; Theatre Arts Books, New York 1968)
White, C. L., *Women's Magazines 1693–1968* (Michael Joseph, London 1970)
White, P., *Poiret* (Studio Vista, London 1973; Potter, New York 1973)
Winterburn, F. H., *Principles of Correct Dress* (New York 1914)

Bibliography of limited-edition magazines

Les Robes de Paul Poiret (Societé Générale d'Impression, for Paul Poiret, Paris 1908)
Les Choses de Paul Poiret (Maquet, for Paul Poiret, Paris 1911)
L'Éventail et la Fourrure (Maquet, for Paquin, Paris 1911)
La Gazette du Bon Ton (Librairie Centrale des Beaux-Art, Paris 1912–25; Condé Nast, N.Y. 1920–25)
Journal des Dames et des Modes (Bureau d'Abonnement, Paris 1912–14)
Modes et Manières d'Aujourd'hui (Pierre Corrard, Paris 1912–22)
Luxe de Paris (G. Heymann, Paris 1913)
La Guirlande des Mois (Librairie Émile Jean-Fontaine & Jules Meynial, Paris 1917–21)
Le Goût du Jour (La Belle Édition, Paris 1918–21)
Les Douze Mois de l'Année (Sauvage, Paris 1919)
Feuillets d'Art (Lucien Vogel, Paris 1919–22)
La Guirlande d'Art et de la Littérature (François Bernourard, Paris 1919–20)
Art, Goût, Beauté (Godde, Bedin, Mondon et Cie, Paris 1920–32)
Dernière Lettre Persane (Fourrure Max, Paris 1920)
The Essence of the Mode of the Day (La Belle Édition, Paris 1920)
Sports et Divertissements (Lucien Vogel, Paris 1920)
Falbalas et Fanfreluches (Éditions Meynial, Paris 1922–26)
Styl (Otto v. Holten, Berlin 1922–24)

Index

Page references to illustrations are printed in *italic* type

Adrian 115
Aghian, Janine *18, 72*
Alix *124*
Allier, Paul *90, 96, 98, 99*
Applied arts *26*, 34, 58, 115
Aprés-midi d'un Faune, L' 51
Arden, Elizabeth 103
Art, Goût, Beauté 26, 28, 69, 94, 98, *106, 108, 110, 111,* 112, *112*
Asquith, Lady Cynthia 66
Aubert 34
Aubusson 121

Bacly *26, 106*
Baguès *71, 90*
Baker, Josephine 86
Bakst, Léon *11,* 18, 38, 43, 52, 56
Baldrich *108, 110, 111*
Balenciaga *124*
Ballet Russe *11*
Ballets Russes 38, *41,* 49, 85
Barbier, George *17, 17, 26,* 28, *50,* 52, *52, 55,* 56, *56, 58, 60, 61,* 64, *64,* 66, *66,* 79, *85,* 86, *89*
Bauhaus 85, *111*
Beauty salon 100, 103
Beer 26, *56, 76*
'Belinda' films *12*
Belle Époque 14, *31, 32, 33,* 37, 49, 58, 76, 100, *102,* 116
Benigni, Leon *94*
Benito *26,* 56, *76*
Bernard 18
Bijoux de Perles, Les 86
Bliss, D. B. 26
Bonfils, Robert *18, 22*
Bow, Clara 115
Boyer *32*
Brocatelles 43
Brock, J. van *50,* 52
Bruhns, Da Silva *71*
Brunelleschi *52,* 69
Bugatti, Carlo 37

Café de Paris 51
Cake Walk 51
Callot Soeurs 33, 37, *89*
Cami-knickers *94, 100*
Carnarvon, Lord 83
Carré, Leon 60
Carter, Howard 83
Cartier *89*
Castle, Irene 51
Castle, Vernon 51
Casque 80

Chanel, Coco 80, 83, 105, 124, *124*
Chansons de Bilitis, Les 28
Chaplin, Charlie *72*
Chefs d'Oeuvre d'Art Japonais 20
Cheruit 36, 55, 56, *117*
Chic 80, 93, 94, 105, 106, *121*
'Chic moderne' 93
Chiffon 31, 46
Chompré *102*
Choses de Paul Poiret, Les 12, 22, 43, *43,* 44, 51, 112
Choses de Paul Poiret vues par Georges Lepape, Les 21
Cito, M. *62*
Cloche 79, 98, *108*
Colbert, Claudette 115
Colcombet *121*
Colette 14
Collette *94*
Collot, Marthe *9, 89*
Condé Nast 62
Congrès Internationaux d'Architecture Moderne (CIAM) 111
Corrard, Pierre 51
Cosmetics 85, 103
Costume Design and Illustration 10
Crêpe de Chine 51, 66, 100
Crépon 51
Crawford, Joan 115
Creed, Henry *122*
Cubism 96
Cubist paintings 71
Cubists 18, 22

Dali, Salvador 98
Dammy, Robert *56*
Dampt 34
Day dresses 74, 80
Décolletage 79, 118, 124
Decorative arts 34, 37, 38, 58, 69, 74, 80, 85, 115, 124
Décorchement, François-Emile 69
Derain 20
Dessau 111
Diaghilev, Serge *11,* 38, 43, 49
Dietrich, Marlene 115, *121*
Dieu Bleu, Le 11
Dinard 79
Dior, Christian 124
'Divan, Le' *102*
Doeuillet 33, 34, 55, *55,* 56
Dory *106*
Doucet 33, 34, *34,* 37, 38, *52,* 56
Douze Mois de l'Année, Les 65
Drecoll *94*
Drian, Étienne *14,* 56, 64
Dufy, Raoul 46, 58, 71
Dunand, Jean 69, 90, 121
Duncan, Isadora 38
Dupas, Jean 121

École des Beaux Arts 20, 26
Eishi *11*
Elégances Parisiennes, Les 65
Elsie, Janice 51
Erté 56, 86; *see also* Tirtoff, Romain de

Essence of the Mode of the Day, The 18, 72
Estampes pour votre chambre 96
Evening dress *14,* 51, *57, 69, 79, 85,* 124

Falbalas et Fanfreluches 28, *79, 85, 89,* 112
Fauré, Camille 71
Fauves 10, 18, 22
Femina 98, 112
Femme Chic, La 98, 112
Femmes Modernes 102
Feuillets d'Art 28, *64,* 66
Feure, de 34
Film fashions 86
First World War 9, *25,* 50, 55, 58, *61,* 62, *65*
Fleurs, Les 90
Fokker XXXVI 124
Folies Bergère 85
Fox trot 51, 74
Furniture 34, 57, 58, 69, 85
Furniture *croquis* 57
Futurists 18

Gaillard 34
Galerie Lutetia *90, 96, 98, 99*
Gallé 34
Garbo, Greta 115
Garters *99,* 100
Gaugin 18
Gazette du Bon Ton 9, *14, 18, 25, 26,* 28, *28, 41,* 52, *55, 55, 56,* 57, *58, 58,* 61, 62, *64,* 65, 69, 71, *71,* 76, *79,* 83, 86, *89, 89,* 112
Gentlemen Prefer Blondes 94
Gibson, Charles Dana 9
Gibson Girls 76
Gide, André 14
Gimpel, René 28
'Gimmy Girl' 102
Glasgow School 37
'Golf, Le' *75*
Gouache 51
Grande Maison de Blanc, La 93, 105
Grands Couturiers 31, 33, 41, 62
Grandes Maisons 41
Gray, Eileen 71
Great War, The 12–14; *see also* First World War
Gross, Valentin 52
Guirlande des Mois, La 28, *58, 60, 61,* 62, 64, 66, *66,* 112

Halouze, Edouard *102*
Harlow, Jean 116, *121*
'Harem pantaloons' 46, 49
Harper's Bazaar 112, *117, 118*
Harper's Bazar 36, 37, 98, 112
Harrison, George *26,* 75
Haute couture 12, 14, 17, 20, 22, 28, 32, 34, 37, *44,* 57, 62, 69, 71, *76,* 116, 118
Hindenburg 124
Hoffmann, Josef 37
Hollywood 86, 102, 105, 115, *115,* 116, 121, *121*
'Hollywood *Déco'* 118
Homme Élégant, L' 26, *75*

Imans, Pierre 64
In Powder and Crinoline 60
Iribe, Paul 10, *12*, 17, 20, 26, 28, 38, *38*, 43, *43*, *44*, 52, *112*
Italian Renaissance 69

Jacquard 31
Jardin des Caresses, Le 60
Jardin des Modes, Le 28
Japanese print *14*, 18, 21
Jazz Age 89
Jenny 69, 89, *106*
'Jet set' *83*
Jewellery 34, 74, 76, 89
Journal des Dames et des Modes 17, 28, *50*, 52, 55, *56*, *112*
Journal des Demoiselles 34

Kabisch, von *86*
Keeler, Ruby 115
Kimono *50*
Kitsch 58, 89
'Knights of the Bracelet' 26

Ladies Magazine 10
La Ferrière 34
Lalique 34
Lamé 31, 46
'Lampshade tunic' 49
Lanvin, Jeanne *28*, 56, *71*, 89, 124
Le Corbusier 96, 98, 111
Leonnel *52*
Lepape, Georges 11, *12*, *14*, 17, 18, 20, 21, 22, 26, 28, *28*, *43*, 44, *44*, *46*, 51, 56, *58*, *61*, 62, 64
Librairie Centrale des Beaux-Arts 52
Lingerie 12, 32
L'Officiel 115
London 22, 32, 38, 51, 57, 60, 61, 62, 65, 79, 100, 105, 116, 121, 124
'London Fashions' 122
'Longchamp' 64
Loos, Anita 94
Louis Seize 66
'Lounge Lizard' 102
Luxe de Paris 28, *52*

Mackintosh 37
MacNairn 37
Madame Matisse 10
Maggie 56
Mainbocher 124
Maisons de couture 56
Manteaux automobiles 38
Marinet, Maurice 69
'Marseillaise, La' *22*
Martial et Armand *34*, *52*, 56, *106*, *110*
Martin, Charles 20, 26, *41*, *49*, 56, *71*, *74*, *75*, *80*, *108*
Martine School of Design 57
Marty, André *9*, *17*, *21*, *25*, 26, 28, *55*, 56, *72*, *73*
Matisse *10*, 17, 20
Maugeant 34
Mère, Clément 69
Metro-Goldwyn-Mayer 86

Meyer, Baron De 66, *117*
Meynial, Jules 66
Modes, Les *31*, *32*, 34, 36
Modes et Manières d'Aujourd'hui *14*, *17*, *21*, *22*, 28, 44, *46*, 49, 51, *52*, 55, *55*, 61, *61*, 62, *72*, *73*, *112*
Modigliani 22
Molyneux 118, 124
Monvel, Bernard Boutet de 26, 28, 56, *57*
Musée des Arts Décoratifs 20

Nadar, Paul 34
New Empire 124
'New Look' 124
New Modernism 85, 89, 90
'New Modernist' 99
New York 32, 34, 38, 51, 57, 61, 62, 79, 105, 118
Nielsen, Kay 60
Nijinsky, Vaslav 51
Normandie 121
Nouvion, Jacques de 52

Odeon Cinemas 121
Offterdinger, Anni *25*
'Oriental Collections' 46

'Panama Pacific International Exhibition' 62
Paquin 33, 34, *34*, 37, *44*, 55, 56, *94*
Paris *10*, 11, *12*, *14*, 17, 20, 22, 28, *28*, 32, *33*, 38, *41*, 51, *52*, 55, 57, 58, 61, *61*, 62, 64, 66, 73, 79, 83, *83*, 100, 105, *105*, 111, *115*, 116, 124
Paris Exhibition of Decorative Arts 86, 93
Paris Exposition Internationale des Arts Décoratifs et Industriels Modernes 86; *see also* Paris Exhibition of Decorative Arts
Patou, Jean *26*, *94*, 105, *106*
Pavillon de l'Élégance 89
Peignoirs 32
Penrose Annual, The 26
Perfume 57, 85
'Persian Celebration' 44
Picasso 18
Pickford, Mary 115
Pichon, Marcelle *76*
Pignet, Robert *115*
Pinet *80*
Pochoir 22, 25, 28, 38, 51, 52, 55, 56, 60, *61*, 66, *112*
Poiret, Madame 46
Poiret, Paul 10, 11, *11*, *12*, *14*, 20, 21, 22, *25*, 38, *43*, *43*, 44, *46*, 46, 49, 55, 56, 57, *112*
Pre-Raphaelites 71, *112*

Quatre Proverbes 100
Quatre Saisons, Les 98, 99
Queen Mary 124
'Qui trop embrasse' 100

'Rah-el-Rah' 62
Rateau, Albert Armand 71, 90
Redfern 33, *41*, 55

Reutlinger *31*, 34
Revue Nègre 86
Ribbons 61
'Riviera, The' 64
Robe de lingerie 55
Robes de Paul Poiret, Les 10, *12*, 20, 38, *38*, *112*
Robes tailleurs 98
Rodier 121
Rojan *93*, *105*
Romme, Martha 56, *64*, *65*
Rubenstein, Helena 103
Ruhlmann, J-E 69, 90, 118
Russian Ballet 18, 38; *see also* Ballet Russe

Salon d'Automne 18, 58
Salon des Arts Décoratifs 58
Saudé, Jean 22, 25, 38, 52, 60, 66
Scheherazade 38, 41
Schiaparelli 98, 123, 124
Schmied, François-Louis 71
Second World War *123*, 124
Shearer, Norma 115
Shimmy 74
Silhouette *9*, *17*, 34, *50*, *52*, *72*, 75, *76*, 76, *86*, 108, *112*, 117, 118, 124
Sports et Divertissements 20, 74, *75*
Stiebel, Victor 116
Styl *25*, 79, *86*
Surrealism 96, 98
Swanson, Gloria 115

Talmadge, Norma *12*
Tango 51, 66, 74
Team illustration 10
Thayaht *83*
Tin Pan Alley 51
Tirtoff, Romain de 86
Tito *100*
Traphagen, Ethel 10
Tulle 65
Turban 22, 44, 46
Turin 37
Turkey Trot 51
Tutankhamun 83

Valentino, Rudolph 96
Vallée 52, 56
Valois, Rose *122*
Vaugirard 52
Vendeuse 32, *34*, 57
Vever 34
'Vichy' 63
Vienna 37
Vionnet, Madelaine 56, *83*, 110, 118
Vitagraph 12
Vogel, Lucien 25, 26, 28, 52, *55*, 69
Vogue 36, 37, 66, 98, 112, *121*

Wall Street 105, *106*, 117
Water Chute, The 20
Workshops 31, *37*
Worth, Jean 17, 33, 38, 55, 56, *57*, 79, *86*, 89, *106*, *108*

Zinoview *89*